rug hooking
with DEANNE FITZPATRICK

rug hooking
with DEANNE FITZPATRICK

Featuring over 40 Distinctively Deanne Rugs
from the past 20 years

Presented by

R·U·G
HOOKING

Published by
AMPRY PUBLISHING LLC
3400 Dundee Road, Suite 220
Northbrook, IL 60062
www.amprycp.com

www.rughookingmagazine.com

Printed in the United States of America

10 9 8 7 6 5 4 3 2 1

On the cover: **So Small Under a Big Sky,** designed and hooked by Deanne Fitzpatrick.

Library of Congress Control Number: 2016943819

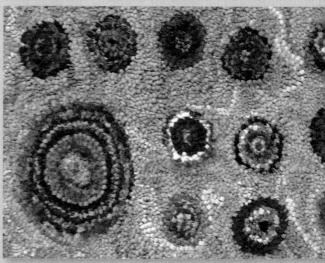

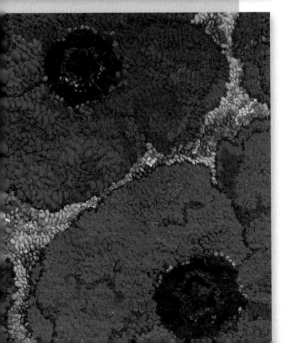

Contents

	Introduction	*vii*
1	Rugs as Art	1
2	The Call of the Sea	7
3	A Rug for Sophie	13
4	Grenfell Mats, Yesterday & Today	17
5	Special Meanings in Rugs	22
6	Élizabeth LeFort Hansford	28
7	Hooking Poppies	34
8	Capturing the Essence	40
9	Letting Light In	47
10	Design 101	54
11	Big Boned Girls	59
12	Giving Back	64
13	Hooking Geometric Rugs	72
14	Twenty Years at the Mat	76
15	Hooking Skies	81
16	Are You a Wild Posy or a Traditional Rose?	91
17	Twenty Tips Learned in Over Twenty Years	98
18	Simply Rug Hooking	103
19	The Rug Hooker's Guide to Creativity	108
	Index of Articles	*117*
	About the Author	*119*

Introduction

For years, as I prepared for workshops or online lessons, I would remember an article I wrote years before and think, "Wouldn't it be great if I had this at my fingertips." So I called *Rug Hooking* magazine and suggested we put together a book of many of the articles I had written for them over the years.

This compendium of my work traces my history as a rug hooker. You can see how my work has evolved and changed over the years into what it is today. I have been hooking rugs for 25 years and hope to be hooking rugs for many more, so at 50 years of age I like to think of this body of work as my first half!

Rug hooking and the community of people that it has brought into my life has been so fine. It has enriched my life and given me an art form and a career. One of the things I have loved about it over the years is the ability to flow from one subject to another. It has been a freestyle ride, learning as I go. My curiosity about design and materials have made it so much fun, and that is what you will see me explore here in this book.

From the firmer form of geometrics to soft flowing fields, I have documented nearly every style or subject I have worked in, and I am thankful for that. Writing has been a big part of my rug-hooking life. Through it I learned about my own process, and writing enables me to examine it and push it a little further. This book is a record of my work: what I learned and what I tried to teach through the pages of the magazine.

It starts from some of my earliest explorations and follows my work over the nearly 20 years that I have had the pleasure of writing for *Rug Hooking* magazine. I hope that at whatever stage in the rug hooking journey you find yourself, you will relate to ideas and inspiration in this book to continue to grow and to hook your own rugs that are both adventurous and beautiful.

Keep hooking—it adds so much to our lives!

—Deanne

Rugs as Art

How to design rugs that reflect your experiences and environment

Designing rugs is exciting and challenging for some people, and a worrisome project for others. All of us, even those who have been designing for years, were once novices in this area of rug hooking.

Often the final product from your first design is a far cry from what you set out to do. Nevertheless, you've taken something personal—a pet, a place, a home, or some treasured object—and transformed it into art, and thus you have arrived at a new level in your work. You are no longer a crafter or an artisan hooking other people's ideas but an artist acting on your own inspiration. Thus, your sense of satisfaction is derived as much from the process as it is from the completed rug.

It Takes Courage

Many people fear stepping over the threshold from working on commercial patterns to creating their own designs. Feeling intimidated by designing is perfectly natural. Few of us feel confident about our artistic abilities and we often spend too much time comparing our talents to those of others. Instead of

using other people's work as inspiration for us to grow from, we allow it to stifle our creativity—the very antithesis of what art is supposed to do.

I gave up drawing when I was eight because I was not as good as my cousin. It wasn't until I learned to hook that I regained my courage to draw. At first it was slow, and I simply adapted other people's images to create new patterns. But as people complimented my rugs I became more daring and began attempting to create more difficult and individualized images.

Famed psychologist Rollo May commented in his book *The Courage to Create* (W.W. Norton & Co., 1994) that we often spend days trying to

Foggy Day in Branch, *34" x 34", #6- and hand-cut wool on burlap. Designed and hooked by Deanne Fitzpatrick, Brookdale, Nova Scotia, 1997. In this piece, Deanne wanted to show the mist over the flattop houses without including the sky.*

Make Me a Channel of Your Peace, *42" x 36", #6- and hand-cut wool on burlap. Designed and hooked by Deanne Fitzpatrick, Brookdale, Nova Scotia, 1997. This piece was hooked in memory of the nuns who served the community where Deanne was raised.*

figure out a problem, only to have the answer come to us weeks later when we've all but forgotten about it. For me, creating rug designs is very much like that. Often I sit in my living room with a large blank piece of burlap strewn across my floor, and my mind is more blank than the burlap in front of me. It was only after I began designing rugs that I could truly understand the concept of writer's block.

Yet there are other times when I drive past a scene that I have passed repeatedly and suddenly the image becomes a rug pattern. I have to agree with May that once you begin to create, ideas stored in the back of your mind arise at the least expected moments. There are times when I can think of no new designs, and other times I am bombarded by so many ideas that many are forgotten before I can sort them out.

Seeking Inspiration

When I feel blank and can think of no new ideas on my own, I seek inspiration anywhere I can. My first step is always to look around my house, which I have filled with my favorite things. If I escape that maze without an idea, I often go through a stack of magazines I have collected over the years. I also look through coffee-table picture books because they are full of unique shots. You would think I would get tired of roaming through the same house and the same books and magazines, but I do not because, as I continue to design and hook, my abilities continue to grow, and that growth gives me more choices.

When I need new stimuli, I borrow books from a friend or purchase new ones, go to a local art gallery, take a drive in the country, or sit with my sketchbook and rethink the images I have already captured.

Sometimes the shade or texture of a piece of wool can trigger an idea. Recently an old plaid jacket in rusts and greens begged to be transformed into an autumn scene as soon as I saw it.

The more I design, the more I draw upon my environment for ideas. One night I was at a concert by the Rankin Family (a group of Cape Breton entertainers), and while there I came up with the idea to hook a fiddler, some women dancing, and a group of musicians. Since that night I have worked on this theme many times and each piece goes a step further. When I go out, I am constantly on the lookout for design ideas without even knowing it.

Drawing from Experience

Beautiful designs also arise from memories and experiences. For example, every time I put a rosebush in a primitive pictorial, I remember the pink roses that Mrs. Edna, a childhood neighbor, grew in her front garden. Each time I hook an ocean scene I feel as if I am kneeling in the front window of my childhood home that overlooked a rocky beach in Placentia Bay, Newfoundland.

Fishwife and Son, *16" x 60", #6- and hand-cut wool on burlap. Designed and hooked by Deanne Fitzpatrick, Brookdale, Nova Scotia, 1997. Cleaning fish in a rural Newfoundland community is the subject of this wallhanging.*

Tips for Designing Rugs

1. Start with something simple so your first effort will be successful.
2. Appreciate the artistic process, prize your rug for being original, and take pride in trying your own design.
3. Always be on the lookout for design ideas. Write them down so you don't forget them.
4. Buy a large, well-bound sketchbook to work out your designs before putting them on burlap. This book also serves as a good record of your designs and a source of inspiration.
5. When you are bored, study the shapes and sizes of objects and how people move. This will help with your drawing.
6. Doodle to your heart's content—it's great practice.
7. Don't worry about perspective. When doing primitives, perspective might intimidate you and hold you back from being really creative.
8. Keep an idea file of photos, magazine clippings, and other visual aids.
9. Be original. Don't be afraid to turn a heart upside down or put a bird where you would least expect it. These things will make your rugs unique.
10. Tell people your design is original when you show them your rug. Praise and encouragement are necessary for your creativity to grow. ▪

The Seven Sisters, *45" x 70", #6- and hand-cut wool on burlap. Designed and hooked by Deanne Fitzpatrick, Brookdale, Nova Scotia, 1997. Deanne and her six sisters are framed by a border of ivy, which symbolizes their close relationship.*

As an adult, I am charmed by the rich culture I am surrounded by here in Cumberland County, Nova Scotia. Inspiration for designs comes from the rocky shores and fishing village of Advocate, the tremendous Bay of Fundy with its rich brown mud, the rolling blueberry hills of Lakelands and Lynn Mountain, the sugar woods, and the great but tragic history of coal mining in Springhill.

On a Sunday drive with my family, it is these things, along with country churches, old farmhouses, hills, and rivers, that we see. Each area has its own beauty and each person his or her own collection of treasured memories. **In** searching for

Autumn in Southhampton, *14" x 80", #6- and hand-cut wool on burlap. Designed and hooked by Deanne Fitzpatrick, Brookdale, Nova Scotia, 1997. Deanne says, "After a drive in the country, I came home and started hooking the marvelous foliage found in Nova Scotia in the fall."*

Rug Hooking Tips
from the Readers of Deanne's Blog

I HAVE KEPT A DIARY or blog on my website for nearly ten years. Most days I write a little something, and we have readers checking in from all over the world. Last year we had over one million page views on my website from over 90,000 people. It is an active and interesting site.

Sometimes I run a little contest on the blog or put out a call for tips and suggestions. These were some of the best tips we received from the rug hookers who read my blog when we had a contest to win a pair of red bloodstone boots.

Don't be a rule-follower. —SA

Invite creative, inspirational hookers and artists to a hooking get-together at your home. Once the group gets together for the first time, the sharing of experience, laughter, and of course hooking will keep the group going. Our weekly hooking group keeps me feeling inspired and hooking. —BM

It's your rug—please yourself. —BP

Tone down the color of your wool by tinting with tea. The shade obtained will depend on the tea variety you use. A weak Earl Grey tea will tint white wool a pinkish beige. Orange pekoe tea will give a yellow/orange hue. I change small pieces of pink wool to flesh tones by soaking in different strengths of tea. —KT

My tip is one that will probably not be too popular with other people you live with: keep your wool and supplies out where you can see them, feel them, and be inspired by them. Keep your wool grouped together by colors and try to do a little bit each day even if it's only 5 or 10 minutes. —AS

Spend less time being in fear of beginning and just begin. All problems are small and correctable once you've started the work. —CV

Just because you have an 18 " strip does not mean you have to hook until you run out—sometimes a few loops adds just the right amount of dash! —NF

Use a hook that will aid and do justice to the connection between the vision in your head and the beauty being created on the burlap. You deserve a hook that has been carefully made, that is visually appealing, and that fits perfectly in your hand. It can be antique or new, cheap or pricey, long or short, fine or stubby. But it has to be The One. —CO

Don't overthink it. I sometimes agonize over the right color or the right width … My suggestion is this: just go with it. The more I hook the better I am at being more relaxed with my thought process. Rug hooking is so forgiving that it always looks wonderful. Don't try to hook like someone else, hook like yourself and then you will enjoy it. —TTC

Listen to the nice ladies at Deanne's studio. They are a wealth of information. —NP

Use the colors you love, but experiment with one other color you might not normally use. Think outside your comfort zone. If you are doing someone's pattern, change one thing in it—be creative. —JB

Whenever you begin a new craft or a new project, buy the best tools and supplies that you can afford. Don't sell yourself short and tell yourself you aren't "good enough" or it's "just practice." Working with quality supplies will make your practice more enjoyable and your end results that much more beautiful. Plus the time you spend on your craft is valuable, and you are worth it! —RS

I always pass along this tip: how to draw a straight line on burlap. Mark your point with a marker and then take a pencil and, with firm pressure, allow the pencil to follow the "ditch." Apply too much pressure and you will slip out of your line. Then darken the line in the same fashion with a marker. —JM

Use your camera to critique your rug. Something that doesn't seem quite right sometimes becomes obvious. —BH

Let nature provide the best cleaning for your rug. Lay your rug face down first and sprinkle snow on it. Then brush the snow off. Do the same on the other side. Then bring it into the house to dry. —KS

Put a few small projects on one piece of backing. They can be about 4 inches apart and you save precious linen. —SM

Put a dryer sheet or similar product under your cutter. It will help to keep the wool fluff under control. —JP

I keep a plastic container on the floor underneath my frame into which I throw the cut-offs. This keeps my work area neat and tidy. It stretches out the time between vacuuming and I love the feel of the snips on my hands when I stir them up! —AD

I recycle the clear zippered plastic bags that blankets come in to hold wool that I've pulled from my stash for a specific rug. Those bags are roomy and you can easily see the contents. The bag keeps things corralled until I'm ready to cut strips again. —PP

I keep a jam jar close at hand to hold scissors, my hook, and the little clipped ends. No more rummaging for my hook among sofa cushions or wool strips. More time to focus on hooking, less on searching for the hook! —AB

I visit yarn shops in search of textured wool yarns in white, cream, oatmeal, grey, or even pale blue, green, pink, or yellow-colored yarns. Then I cut the yarns into 3-4 yard lengths. I toss these into my dye pot along with whatever I am dyeing. Sometimes I crunch the yarn together or lay it across multiple colors, or spoon various colors over it. This process yields great colored textures to use with my wools. —AM

I find color inspiration for rug hooking every day, whether it is thumbing through magazines, looking at nature, or walking through a store. –LG ■

designs, our own experience can be our greatest inspiration.

Remember that creativity is not an event. It is a process. Our designs will naturally grow and change as we do. They evolve out of our experiences, our cultural heritage, the landscape around us, and the stimuli in which we immerse ourselves. How well we draw does not matter. When we look at some of the antique rugs that grace the floors of museums, it is often their primitiveness, rather than their perfection, that charms us.

Those of you who want to design rugs must jump right in. If your ideas are too lofty, your experience and ability will tone them down. Where would we be if the early settlers had waited for stamped patterns? My grandmother, in outport Newfoundland, used a piece of charred wood from the fire to draw onto burlap bags. Today we have many tools—silk screens, markers, tracing pencils and papers, and fine Scottish burlap. Yet we sometimes rely very little on the most important tool at our disposal—our own creativity.

The Call of the Sea

Stormy or calm, the sea is everchanging

"Call me Ishmael." Well, maybe not. I'd like to say I am an old salt but I am not. I grew up overlooking the water and went with my father to buy fish right off the boat, but my knowledge of the sea is all gained from watching it. I was 12 the first time I crossed the sea on a ferry to leave my island home, Newfoundland. I was 15 before I had a proper boat ride across the bay in a skiff.

People who grow up on islands often have a special relationship with the sea because they are surrounded by it. They know it from watching it, and that is how I know the water. I loved to watch boats cross the bay, the capelin fish roll in on the beach, and see the big breakers crash against and climb over the beach rock seawall at Argentia. It was always so interesting: the movement, the changing color, the shape. I could watch it for hours.

Our house was a plain three-story house on a hill overlooking Freshwater Beach. I would lean against the back of a chair in the middle window on the second floor and watch who was going up and down the hill and watch the water. I was as curious and inquisitive then as I am now.

I live on a much different shore now than the huge thunderous Placentia Bay where I grew up. The Northumberland Strait is a perfectly blue, mostly calm, tidal water that empties out twice a day—leaving big sand flats for miles around. You can walk in that water for a long way before it is deep, and it is said to be the warmest water north of the Carolinas. It does not seem dangerous or

March Sails, *50" x 58", 2016.*

Waves Rise Up to Meet You, *each 22" x 36", 2009.*

ominous like the waters I grew up near. If I had not sat in my window and watched helicopters search for three lost fisherman I would not believe that the strait could rear its ugly head and be as much to be feared as the big Atlantic. It is serene, but it too is a powerful force to be reckoned with. Living on the water I have learned to respect it. As beautiful as it is, I know it is not to be fooled with, even when it looks calm and peaceful.

I think back to how my grandfathers must have felt on the water in a dory off the coast of Newfoundland. There is a famous Breton fisherman's prayer, "Oh God, thy sea is so great and my boat is so small." This little prayer sums up our

relationship with the water and is no doubt a metaphor for life. President John F. Kennedy, famous for his use of quotes, kept a bronze plaque of it on his desk in the Oval Office.

Many artists are drawn to the water as a theme, and rug hookers are no different. In rug hooking we can take control of the sea in a way that we never could in a little boat, or even in a great ship. First of all, we get to determine that other great force of nature—the weather—when we hook. I am not kidding. It is the weather that determines what our sea will look like. Once after riding a ferry across Placentia Bay to South East Bight, a tiny community reachable only by boat, I came back to my bed and breakfast excitedly announcing how blue the water was. My host, a painter herself, asked, "What color was the sky?" Of course, it was blue as well. Under a blue sky the sea is even bluer. Under a grey sky it picks up the grey. So the first thing to think about as you hook the sea is not a lot different from the first thing a fisherman considers before he boards his boat:

"What is the weather like?"

"What color is the sky?"

"Is the wind up or is it a calm day?"

The answers to these questions will inform you about the color and texture you'll use in the sea.

There are two main types of water that I hook in my rugs: calm water and stormy seas.

Stormy Seas

Let's start with a stormy sea. You may want to choose some grimy ocean-coast colors. Being used to the Atlantic Ocean, you would be looking for greys, dark blues, and even muddy aqua colors. You will also need lots of creams, whites, and pale yellows to accent the tops of the waves. In the creams you might want some fleece or yarns to accent the excitement of the waves. When I hook this kind of water, I hook across, but in jagged and rough lines. I will almost shake my hand as I hook so that the hooked lines are looser and non-conformist. What you are really hooking is the effect the wind has on the water—you are imagining how the wind is blowing and hooking the lines in that direction. Look for interesting tweeds that have blues or aquas with flecks of grey, cream, or white in them to mix with the water colors. This will give the effect of sea spray and enhance the windy feeling.

Swim Sisters, *20" x 16", 2012.*

From Sea to Sky, *48" x 42", 2010.*

Calm Water

I find this the hardest to hook because there is little room for movement or color change. You know how I love to add texture and color to my rugs. When I hook this sort of sea I have to exercise control. I pick some dark to medium blues and hook across the mat with a slight ripple. I choose blues that are quite close in color because, when the sun is shining full and bright, there are not a lot of color variations in the water. I do not use a lot of texture in these rugs. I might use a plain yarn along with some wool cloth, but this is not the place for curly locks or lots of fleece. You want fairly smooth yarns and cloth for a smooth sailing sea, and you want to hook it in the same manner.

Sometimes I like hooking the ocean in a playful way. I forget all about the reality of the sea and hook the water from my imagination. This is a more abstract approach and it takes a creative bent to let go of how you have seen the sea for years and turn it into something else altogether. This approach is not about hooking the sea as it really is—it is about making a rug that is decorative and beautiful and makes you feel the sea. Think of all the elements of the sea . . . coral, starfish, fish, bubbles, waves, rocks, foam, seaweed, shells, driftwood, snails, tiny fish, shellfish, sandbars, sun hats, bathing suits, lawn chairs, flip flops, umbrellas. Now imagine throwing all these things in a bag and pulling out a few and designing a sea rug. You can get the feeling of the sea and summer in many ways with any of these elements.

The Embellished Sea

Sometimes I embellish the water with paisleys, circles, fish, circles, etc. Once I start on this type of sea

I am in the land of my imagination. The fish could be any color. The paisleys might be dark teardrops or they might be bright colorful sparks of life under the sea. Basically all I am doing is playing with a large area and adding some interest and fun. This whole idea started when I saw a dinner napkin at my sisters' home. The artist had taken all the areas of the landscape and used them as areas to decorate, adding shapes to the different sections. Shortly after that, I began seeing the sea in my rugs as a place to create. When I sketch on the rug I will draw in the designs, and I often begin by hooking these areas first. I sometimes use colors that are close to the water for these elements, but other times I will pull colors from other areas of the rug and begin there by outlining a paisley or circle. I then hook each one separately, as if there was no relation between them. I do not worry about them all being the same. Sometimes I will even add some crazy colors, like lime green or bright yellow, just to make them stand out a bit more. I will fancy one up with a sparkly yarn and dull another one down with a grey tweed.

Once all the embellishments are hooked, I start on the background. If I want the embellishments to blend in, I will hook the background in a similar shade. To make them stand out, I hook it in a contrasting shade. Sometimes, for example, I will hook around the circles while other times I will hook right up the left side of the circle, then hook on the right side of it. This method means that the background will look as if the circles are laying on top and the background is going through the circle from behind.

The Stylized or Semi-Abstract Wave

Some of my sea rugs are all about the wave. Either the wave is really large in the foreground—as if it were a tidal wave—or it is the whole rug itself. In these situations, the whites and creams you use are as important as the colors you choose for the sea itself. I have made a dozen rugs in this genre and

I have dozens more to make. This style of rug is all about "feeling" the sea and expressing your feelings in an abstract way through color and texture.

There are two main areas in these rugs: the wave crests and the background areas. In the wave crests I use whites and creams, but that is just my choice. The palest shades of any color could work. In the backgrounds, I have experimented mostly with blues and mauves, but there is room here to play. Choose your own palette and see how it works out. What would happen if you chose greens? Could it still work as a wave? That will depend on all the shades you use and how abstract you want to get with your work.

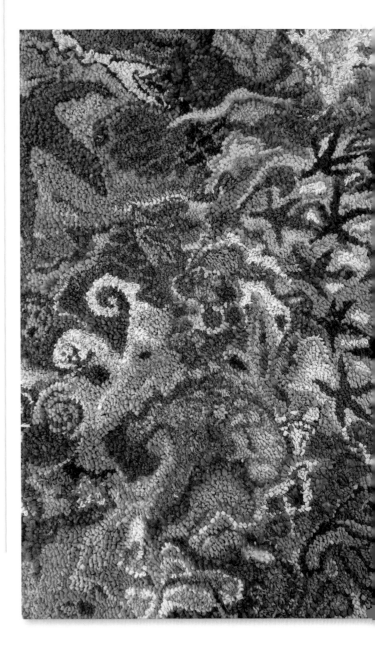

Beach Path, *30" x 64", 2014.*

→ Thick bars of creams, whites, lots of texture in the wave crest

← The background areas could all be the same or each could be a different colour

I also like to throw in a few teardrops, circles, or other shapes in these rugs, depending on how big they are, so that there are some areas of interest in the rug that draw the viewer in.

Sea Stories

There is no one way to hook the sea, and the ideas I have shared with you here are not "the" way to hook the sea. I like to think that you will use these ideas and the images shown here to chart your own course in hooking the sea. I am drawn to do it a certain way but I am always looking for new ways, new materials, new colors, and new textures to make my sea rugs better. Most recently I rode on a sailboat in the Caribbean Sea, and that experience has lead me to hook the sea in a whole new way. I sat right under the sails for two hours as we set off towards an uninhabited island. I did not have my camera with me, so I borrowed my friend's camera and shot the sails. As soon as we got home I started nagging her for the photos because I had this great desire to create a rug design. The sea rug I am working on now has none of the Caribbean colors that you might imagine I would choose. Instead, to create the rug, I chose the colors that calm me because the rug is not only about the sea and sailing; it is about the feeling I had sitting under those sails, a feeling of contentment.

Hooking the water

calm water

movement in water

stylized wave

rougher water

decorative wave

Most sea rugs have an element of story to them. As you go about hooking your rug, make sure you include your story and choose the colors that remind you of the feeling you had as you watch the waves roll in. Create a rug that is as rich and full of life as the sea itself.

A Rug for Sophie

----

*Commemorating a special life
in a hooked rug*

There is a lot that goes into making a rug from recycled clothing. The garment must be torn apart, washed and dried, cut into thin strips, and hooked loop by loop into backing. Most of us think about our lives as we hook: the things that weigh heavily on us and the things that lighten our hearts. With each loop we pull, we dream a little dream. A rug can be a celebration of life or a memorial to a life cut short.

Sophie North

I sit here writing this story with a heavy heart. Having spent the day celebrating my son's sixth birthday with 12 of his friends, I can't help but think of little Sophie North, the subject of a rug I was asked to hook. She celebrated far too few birthdays.

A Fortuitous Encounter

On a cold, wet day in the early summer of 1997, Mick North and Sandra Uttley dropped by my studio for a visit. We enjoyed each others' company for a couple of hours. Over tea and muffins I taught Sandra how to hook, and she and Mick bought two rugs for their new home in Scotland. Each year several hundred people stop by my studio when they are visiting Nova Scotia, and each

visitor is memorable in some way, but Sandra and Mick stood out that summer. They were people I could easily have been friends with if we had had more time to spend together.

Nearly six months later, in mid-December, I came in from getting my mail. I shook the snow off my boots and sat down to read the Christmas cards that had come. An envelope from Scotland caught my eye and I opened it first. Inside I discovered pictures of the rugs Sandra and Mick had bought, and I was delighted that they were thoughtful enough to send them so I could see where the rugs were hung in their home. But as I read the short letter inside I was overcome with sadness and started to cry. Donna Farrel, my friend who works with me, asked what was wrong. I said, "My God, Dunblane. Remember Dunblane?"

As I read the note I learned that Mick had lost his only daughter, five-year-old Sophie, in March 1996 when a gunman had stormed into Sophie's primary school in Dunblane, Scotland, and had shot her and 15 other schoolchildren as well as their teacher. This personal tragedy of Mick's was compounded by the earlier loss of Sophie's mother, who had died of breast cancer in 1993. Sandra and Mick's letter said they wanted to commission a rug in memory of Sophie. Reading their note made real for me an event that until that moment had simply been a news item on television.

At first I felt I could not do it. I was fearful of the emotions I would face as I worked with Mick and Sandra. At the time my own children were one and four years of age. Working on this project would force me to face the reality that no matter how hard I tried, I could not protect my children from all the dangers in the world. We all know this intellectually, but as a new mother it was difficult for me to accept emotionally.

At the same time, I knew there was no way I could not be part of making a rug in memory of Sophie. Mick and Sandra's gentle invitation to become a part of their life and share their grief was heartfelt and deep. I believed that in some way making this rug might be helpful to them, and I knew it would be meaningful for me.

Designing a Tribute

At first we communicated by mail, then later by fax. Through the letters and pictures I learned that Sophie, whom Mick referred to as his little sunflower, was spirited and loved to draw. They sent pictures of her bedroom, the view from her window, her house, and her community. I learned that an early spring bulb had been named after Sophie by a horticulturist friend of Mick's, and that the same flower, the snowdrop, had become the symbol of the anti-gun campaign in Britain. Mick and Sandra were active in this campaign, and Mick had started a newsletter about it. Since Sophie's death he had retired from his teaching job and was working full-time on the newsletter.

The design for the rug developed as I read the letters from Sandra and Mick. I thought about what they told me about Sophie and the community she lived in. As I learned more about her and her life, themes and ideas emerged—the sunflowers and snowdrops seemed to be the perfect symbols for the child. The delicate snowdrop, which emerges in the early spring and was one of the few flowers blooming when the tragedy took place, was symbolic of the fragility of life. The sunflower, with its glorious but brief beauty, seemed to represent Sophie's short existence. Though her time on earth had been brief, she had had a strong and beautiful impact on those around her. I asked if it would be all right to include her image in the rug and Mick readily agreed, so I have her peeking out between sunflowers. Mick and Sandra liked the idea of a shaped mat like some I had done previously. We determined the measurements based on where they wanted to hang the rug in their home, and decided on a shaped rug measuring about 50" x 28."

I faxed some rough sketches to Mick and Sandra, and once we agreed on the basic elements of the design, I began to draw it on primitive burlap. The rug grew from the initial sketch, but the original concept remained unchanged. I drew the outlines of Sophie, the sunflowers, the snowdrops, the border, and the village of Dunblane. Rather than draw in all the details, I hooked them in a freestyle manner as I made the rug. The rug was hooked in a #6 cut and some hand-cut wool. (I like to incorporate

Detail of Sophie's Rug

Sophie's Rug, *48" x 28", #6-cut and hand-cut wool on burlap. Designed and hooked by Deanne Fitzpatrick, Amherst, Nova Scotia, 1998. Deanne hooked this rug as a memorial to Sophie North, who was killed in a school shooting in Scotland.*

some hand-cut wool into all my work. Not only does it create a nice effect, but I like the personal touch it adds to a rug.)

Loops Mixed With Tears

The entire rug was hooked with recycled fabric, all at least 80 percent wool. One thing I regretted was not having some personal clothing of Sophie's or her family's to hook into the mat. I think that makes a memorial rug even more meaningful.

Some of the fabric was used as is and some was dyed. The green for the hills and the petals of the snowdrops was dyed in my usual fashion—I mixed a bit of this-and-that dye in a cup of hot water and then poured it into a pot on the stove. I could not repeat those colors, just as I could not repeat Sophie's rug. Tweeds were used to create

the effect of stone in the background buildings. Bits of mauve were hooked into the green along the riverbank to represent the rhododendrons that grow in the village of Dunblane.

I wanted the sky to have a heavenly feeling, so I used four shades of light blue and hooked them in random patches, with large patches of white for the clouds. The stained glass windows in the cathedral were created by hooking one or two loops of a color and then clipping the strip. By packing 8 or 10 colors into a small area, you can create the effect of stained glass. For Sophie's smiling face and the background of the border I used several shades of tan or camel. The border background was hooked in random patches. I used three shades of yellow from blankets for the petals of the sunflowers. Pale yellow, strong gold, and bright yellow worked well together to create a primitive shaded effect. For the sunflowers' centers I mixed several dark brown tweeds to create the appearance of the seeds.

As I hooked the rug I kept thinking about the little girl who had been lost. More tears fell between the loops of that rug than of any other I had made. As I pulled each loop through the backing, I thought about Sophie's short but significant life, the family she left behind, and my own family. I reminded myself about the importance of wanting what you have instead of chasing rainbows. Making the rug turned into a kind of therapy for me, a chance to think about my own life while sharing another family's grief.

This was the first time I had hooked a memorial rug. The best part of the project was the dialogue that took place between Sophie's family and me. Through this project I gained a special relationship. Making the rug was more about loss and suffering through a difficult time than it was about finding the right wool or the right cut. The design was the most significant part of making the rug because it had to be not only my representation of Sophie, but also Mick's representation. He was her father, who knew and loved her, and I needed to reflect the things he thought were important. In making this rug I took second stage as the artist. I needed to be willing to communicate in wool the stories Sandra and Mick were telling me, not my own stories. It was the most meaningful rug I have ever made, and my heart breaks a little every time I think about it. This endeavor is not something I could repeat.

As soon as I finished the rug I shipped it to Scotland. Mick and Sandra received it the day after the second anniversary of Sophie's death. They wrote back, "The rug has arrived! It is absolutely beautiful. Perfect. We put it up on the wall straightaway. I wish you could see it here. I know one day you will. As soon as I saw it, I thought of Sophie 'still smiling somewhere,' [as it says] on her headstone."

I was relieved that they were happy with the rug. As much as I did the rug for them, I had also done it for myself and my own family. I put my heart and soul into it, letting myself grieve for a little girl I had never known. And, in the end, perhaps that emotional bond is the essence of what we do as rug hookers. A rug is more than the sum of its parts. What we put into it of ourselves is what gives it meaning—and what makes it art.

Grenfell Mats, Yesterday & Today

These now-prized pieces once saved a province

Hooking mats (rugs) was a well-established craft in northern Newfoundland by the time Sir Wilfred Grenfell arrived on its rugged seacoast at the end of the nineteenth century. Under his influence, what was once a necessary household task became a thriving cottage industry that helped to put Canada's easternmost provinces on the map. Today those same mats are again proclaiming the skill of those early rug hookers.

Wilfred, a young English doctor, arrived in 1892 to find terrible hardship in Newfoundland. Born in 1865 in the village of Parkgate, England, Wilfred studied medicine in London. Initially he worked in the slums of London and later provided medical help for fishermen on the North Sea. After three years of this work he responded to a call for doctors to serve the fishermen of northern Newfoundland and Labrador.

Upon his arrival, Wilfred began what would become a lifelong service to the people of these Atlantic provinces. The inhabitants of the region were largely destitute; malnutrition had led to scurvy, tuberculosis, and other ailments. Fishermen could barely keep their families fed and were often taken advantage of by the merchants and traders who bought their fish. Wilfred's medical mission to the coast of Labrador was a welcome one. His first hospital was established in Battle Harbour in 1893. By 1900 construction had begun on a hospital in St. Anthony, and three years later it was serving 25 communities.

Wilfred was impressed with the strong, welcoming people he met on the coast. He was convinced that teaching the people how to help themselves would be better for them than charity. This led him to form the Industrial Department of the Grenfell Mission, a cottage handicrafts industry, in 1906.

Some Grenfell mats depicted religious subjects, such as this stained-glass portrait.

Birth of an Industry

The idea for "the Industrial" was born in the spring of 1905, when Wilfred met Jessie Luther while on a lecture tour in Massachusetts. Jessie had pioneered the use of arts and crafts as therapy for nerve problems, and had set up such a program in Rhode Island. Upon learning of this, Wilfred thought that a craft such as weaving could supplement the incomes of the people he was working with. During the summer of 1906, Jessie trekked to St. Anthony to work at the Industrial. During the first few years the focus of the industry was on weaving, but the need for special equipment, an inconsistent supply of wool, and the lack of local skill made it difficult for the fiber craft to flourish.

By 1908, it was recognized that mat hooking offered greater potential than weaving for a cottage industry. Women did not need any training—they already hooked mats as their mothers and grandmothers had done before them. Each home had all the supplies needed: a frame, a hook, wool and cotton scraps, and burlap feed bags. Jessie and

A colorful Grenfell mat depicting mallards in flight.

A dog sled scene, typical of Grenfell mats.

Wilfred realized that the mats could be sold in the United States to fund the Mission.

The birth of the Grenfell hooked mats was recorded in Jessie's journal, dated January 29, 1908: "This afternoon was the beginning of the matting circle. Several women came but evidently with the idea of looking around before committing themselves. The women quickly learned that the mats they hooked could be traded in at the Industrial for cash, clothing, or food vouchers." Wilfred supervised the sale of the mats in the United States, and mat hooking quickly became the mainstay of the Industrial, with the majority of the 2,000 handicraft workers registered as mat hookers.

Supplies and Materials

Women were given their supplies in kit form, with a pattern printed on burlap, or brin. The most common theme among the patterns were northern scenes of fishing, hunting, animals, and dog sleds. They were color keyed and hooked carefully. Wilfred's wife, Anne, standardized the mats. The most

recognizable trait of the Grenfell mats is that they were almost always hooked in horizontal lines, with sometimes as many as 200 loops per square inch. Quality was strictly controlled. At first the mats were made with wool and cotton, but by 1928 they were hooked with silk and rayon.

To meet the demand for mats, the mission solicited donations of discarded silk stockings from the south. In America, the slogan "When your stockings run, let them run to Labrador" got a great response. Middle-class and wealthy Americans would pack up their old stockings to send to the mission. The stockings' light jersey texture was perfect for dyeing in pretty pastels and comfortable for hooking. Finely woven burlap was purchased in large bolts by the mission. Used X-ray film from Wilfred's hospitals was cut into stencils to transfer the designs onto burlap.

Each Friday the mats were brought to the mission by the hookers. The most common mat size

Note the horizontal hooking in this portrait of the popular sled dog. Straight-line hooking is a characteristic of Grenfell mats.

was 25" x 41". The mats were generally sold for $5 to $10, with part of the fee going to the hooker and part to the Industrial. For example, if a mat was sold for $8.50, $5 went to the artist and $3.50 to the Industrial. Of course, all the money made by the Industrial was invested into the community to purchase supplies and support the hospitals. The mat making was a godsend to the women; it was their first opportunity to make money and escape some of the debt that burdened them. In the early years, less than 200 mats were made; at the peak of productivity, more than 3,000 mats were hooked. Boutiques in Philadelphia, New York, and Boston sold the products of the Grenfell Mission. In Canada, Grenfell mats had their own section in Eaton's department stores. The Great Depression led to a drop in the sale of mats, and interest in the industry declined dramatically after World War II. Wilfred died in 1940.

Color and Design

To briefly describe Grenfell mats as northern scenes would diminish the character and beauty of the wonderful designs. Before the Industrial's influence, women had generally been hooking geometric or floral patterns. Stamped patterns were creeping into some Newfoundland homes but had to be purchased; they were not a priority in a hungry household.

Initially most designs were created by Wilfred or Jessie, but as time went on many other people, including the hookers themselves, designed patterns. The designs reflected the social and cultural history of the area as well as the work ethic of the region's people. The earliest patterns showed dog sleds, bears on the snow, or geese in flight. Other patterns included schooners, walruses, churches, icebergs, spear hunting, drying salt cod, and seagulls flying over a lighthouse. All the designs related to the life of the women who hooked them, which is one of the wonderful things about Grenfell mats. It would have been easy to try to make the designs more marketable in the United States by hooking motifs that reflected the American way of life. Instead, the designers chose to reflect the cultural traditions of the area in which they were working.

One designer, Rhoda Dawson, offered new inspiration in the 1930s. Her designs were sophisticated, somewhat abstract, and sometimes designed to be hooked in the subtle shades of undyed stockings. These mats are rare today, as they were less popular with the hookers, who liked to work with brighter shades, and with the public, who had become used to northern scenes.

Renewed Interest

Although the last Grenfell mats were produced in the 1940s, they are enjoying a resurgence of interest and popularity today. Paula Laverty, who has collected, researched, and written about Grenfell mats, says she "either has a passion or a serious problem. I devoted the last 17 years of my life to [these mats]." Her work has contributed a great deal to the renewed interest in Grenfell rugs, which are now valuable and sought after. Rugs that once sold for $5 to $8 may now be worth between $3,000 and $8,000, depending on their subject, availability, and condition.

Robin Moore purchased more than 120 Grenfells in the course of 20 years. Her collection recently appeared for sale at an art show in Ontario for $300,000. It has reportedly been sold, although no one is telling who bought it. Although collections like this one are rare, Paula estimates there are "thousands of [Grenfell] rugs around today."

Paula has worked hard to bring the Grenfell mats to the public. In 1994 she was a guest curator for Northern Scenes: Hooked Art of the Grenfell Mission at the prestigious Museum of American Folk Art in New York City, and in 1996 she was the curator of the Silk Stockings mat show at the Shelburne Museum in Shelburne, Vermont. Paula recently was in charge of another show, Matting Season, at the Museum of Textiles in Toronto. This exhibit was her greatest effort yet. There were 106 mats depicting a wide range of the patterns hooked at the mission, brought together from various private and corporate collections. In addition to the familiar scenes there were florals, sea urchins, and starfish, as well as Rhoda Dawson's work. The symbols and motifs contained in the works depicted not only the climate, flora, and fauna of the region, but also the hard-working nature of the people, their religion, and their lifestyle in the early part of this century. The soft muted shades so typical of Grenfell mats were interspersed with rich rust and brown florals that were less familiar. The Matting Season is a touring exhibit; dates and locations are listed on Paula's website at *www.grenfellhookedmats.com*.

The tradition of mat making continues today at Grenfell Handicrafts in St. Anthony, now a privately owned company. Many of the traditional patterns are still hooked, with yarn, by local hookers. The Grenfell Historical Society takes an active part in community life, and 60 years after the good doctor's death, Wilfred Grenfell remains a household name.

Special Meanings in Rugs

There's more than wool in many a rug

Last winter I had a lot of changes in my life. My father, who had struggled for years with a debilitating illness, died in February. As lonely as it made me to have him leave this world, I felt a great sense of relief for him when he had drawn his last breath. He was 79 and had been languishing in a nursing home for five years. My father's spirit had been gone for a long time. In his illness he had become less than a shadow of his former self. He had not recognized or spoken to me for more than two years. This was quite something for a man who had been a robust storyteller, sitting at the kitchen table with friends and a drink. After my father died I came home from the nursing home and spent a lot of time thinking about him. I struggled to understand why I was grieving.

Two months later, I lost my mother suddenly and unexpectedly. She had a heart attack getting out of her bath. By the time I got to the hospital she was gone. She was a fine woman, a hard worker. The loss of both parents in such a short time made me reflect on the stories surrounding my life with them. I came to understand that stories can be told through wool, and in the telling they can take on new life.

Gathering Stories

My childhood was rich with stories, thanks to my family and my community. I grew up on the island of Newfoundland next to the American naval base at Argentia. Our community always had strong ties with the United States, not only because of the Americans who lived nearby, but also because many local girls married Navy men and moved with them to the States. They would send home parcels filled with used clothing and treats that could not be bought in our local stores, like Rice-a-Roni.®

Newfoundlanders also had a strong tradition of working on the high steel in New York City. Local boys who had grown up balancing themselves in dories on the rough Atlantic Ocean found they were well suited to walking across two-foot steel girders 20 stories above Manhattan. If you lost your balance in either case the effect would have been the same, and chances of survival were grim.

When I was little, some of the most exciting times at our house were when these friends and relatives arrived from the States for summer vacation. This was story time in our house. As people came and went, the stories got longer and the characters grew larger than life. Aunts, uncles, and neighbors gathered around our kitchen table where they ate, drank, and told tales.

In the time since my parents' death I have come to realize that many of the stories that have been told in my hooked mats I learned through them. I never hauled a net from the rough Atlantic waters, or salted a fish for market, but I watched and listened well.

Seven for a Secret Never Told, *52" x 68", #6- and #8-cut and hand-cut wool on burlap. Designed and hooked by Deanne Fitzpatrick, Amherst, Nova Scotia, 2000.*

We as rug hookers can gather stories today the same way my parents did, by sharing what we have. The people who visited us every summer knew that in my parents' house there was a warm seat, a cold beer, homemade bread, and a bottle of jam. They knew they would hear a tale or two, and that their story would be heard. As much as people like to hear other's stories, they are often dying to tell their own. Sharing your life with others is the easiest and most natural way to gather stories. Being open to the moment, offering a hand, and asking the right questions can lead to the most amazing discoveries.

The other thing to remember is a story is just that—a story. A friend of mine who is a writer says the story is more important than the truth, and I have to agree. It is the integrity of the story, not necessarily the factual truth, that counts. Stories can be factual or fictitious, fantasy or myth. You must decide what you want to tell. The story is up to you.

Keeping a journal is an easy way to record your stories. A journal allows you to explore the stories you might like to tell in a hooked rug. You can recount daily activities and past events, both big and small.

Family pictures, especially old ones, can lead to all sorts of ideas for hooked mats. When I look at an old photograph, I always wonder about the circumstances on the edge of the picture, the part I cannot see. Who took the picture? What lies behind the picture? Asking yourself these questions are great fodder for your imagination, especially if you are not worried about the truth. The picture, just like a good pictorial mat, gets the mind going—even though the viewer is only given a hint of the real story.

Let Your Rugs Speak

Once you have decided that you want to tell a story with your rug, and you have decided on the story, what's next? The adage "A picture paints a thousand words" is true enough, but how can a picture make us experience an emotion or think something? How does it lead us to believe or question something about ourselves?

A picture, painting, or hooking is a way of communicating. The artist is communicating something to everyone who looks at it. Sylvia Plath, the famous American poet and author of *The Bell Jar*, once said that after she wrote a poem she left it to the reader to interpret it. Good art is like that. The fiber artist sets out to say one thing, but another may be interpreted. That happens because each of us views the rug from our own experience. Thus when we set out to tell a story in a rug we cannot control the responses to it. In some cases, visitors to my studio had interpretations of my rugs that were more interesting than my own. We should be willing to listen to other views of our rugs, as they can sometimes give us a glimpse of our inner selves. I am not always in touch with my emotions or ideas, yet they come out in my rugs. This is a delightful, but not a common, way of having a story emerge from a rug.

Storytelling can be much more deliberate than this. We can set out to make our rugs narrative pictorials. I tell a lot of different kinds of stories in my rugs. Sometimes they are strict narratives of a factual event and other times they are facts embellished with a bit of fiction.

What is it you have to tell? Look at your own life, your experiences, and your surroundings. Sometimes when I am working with a group of people, I have each person create a life line. Each one takes a large piece of paper and draws a line on it, putting at its beginning a zero and at its end her present age. Along the line they draw pictures or write notes about the important events in their

Something in Common, *48" x 66", #6- and #8-cut and hand-cut wool on burlap. Designed and hooked by Deanne Fitzpatrick, Amherst, Nova Scotia, 2000.*

PHOTO COURTESY CHRIS REARDON

The Meaning of the Journey, *50" x 48", #6- and #8-cut and hand-cut wool on burlap. Designed and hooked by Deanne Fitzpatrick, Amherst, Nova Scotia, 2000.*

lives. You can try this too, to discover the stories in your own past.

The Elements of Your Rug

Once you have decided on your rug's story, you need to figure out its important elements. Do they include people, places, or things? Will there be symbolism in the design or words in the border?

One of my rugs, *Too Many Boats in the Water*, started out being a beautiful pictorial of a seaside village. As I began to draw, the news came on the radio that the Supreme Court of Canada

had granted fishing rights to a native man who had been charged with illegal fishing. The story shook me. I knew that something important was happening, and I decided to tell that story in my mat. The fishery in Atlantic Canada had once been the mainstay of our economy, but in recent years, with declining fish stock, catches were low and some areas had been put under a moratorium, meaning that fishermen were no longer allowed to fish. I knew that this decision would cause a lot of friction. I worked out my concerns in the rug.

I created a typical coastal village, facing all the houses toward the water. In the foreground and

Too Many Boats in the Water, *72" x 68", #6- and #8-cut and hand-cut wool on burlap. Designed and hooked by Deanne Fitzpatrick, Amherst, Nova Scotia, 1999.*

background I put in many boats, symbolizing the stress on the fishery. I also put two groups of people (one in red shirts to symbolize the natives and the other in white shirts to symbolize the white fishermen) having a tug of war. At the very top of the rug I wrote a line from an old fishing song: "There is a place where the fishermen gather." When you first look at this rug you might see just a village, but if you take few minutes you can see the layers of meaning.

Sometimes a rug can be used to state a belief. I had spent years as a counselor assisting people with depression, and I wanted to create a rug about the experience. I believe we spend too much time searching for answers and not enough time enjoying our daily life. Thus I created the rug *The Meaning of the Journey*. In it I created another idyllic coastal village. In the foreground I had people dancing as if at a garden party, and at the top of the rug I wrote, "The meaning of the journey is between you and me." What I meant is that people should have fun, enjoy the present, and take notice of who is on the journey of life with them. I believe that in others we find meaning.

In both of these rugs I used words to write message in the rug. I did this by hooking words in double rows so they would be readable. I also hooked them in a color that stood out from the background. Writing words in your rug is a clear and direct way of helping the viewer understand your story.

A border can be important in a story rug. It is a great place to write a message, set down a date or place, or use a motif or symbol that is important to the narrative. The border in another rug I hooked became a vital element in telling a tale.

Although Atlantic Canada has undergone an economic crisis with the loss of its fishery, its residents are a resilient people who know how to make do. This is the story I wanted to tell in *Seven for a Secret Never Told*, because we never hear much about what happens to people who lose their jobs due to a change in a country's economy. The media forgets about them after a year or so, but they are still out there making a living one way or another. What happens to them and how they survive is often a neglected story. In this rug I used the border to add seven blackbirds to the mat. According to folklore, seven blackbirds symbolize a secret never told. In the body of the mat I put five different kinds of workers standing under the night sky. A woman is holding a codfish to signify the importance of fish in the story. The man is holding a gaff, which is a hook for catching fish.

When you feature a person in your rug, let what he or she is wearing or holding help tell the tale. The person's clothes, hat, boots, and accessories (such as the fisherman's gaff) reveal who the person is. It is these little things that describe character and lead the viewer to think about the person in a certain way.

Symbols are a great way of telling stories. Many books describe the symbolic meaning of flowers and animals, and others explain the decorative symbols found in many cultures, such as Celtic, Arabic, Egyptian, and Roman. I often use traditional floral, scroll, and leaf borders on rugs that are more pictorial and contemporary in design. I like to mix old-fashioned traditional borders with contemporary designs to show respect for the history of rug hooking.

The wool you use in the rug can also be part of the story of the rug. My rug *Something in Common* was created from the wool donated by 77 women who had survived breast cancer. Joan Stephenson sent a piece of wool from a suit of her mother's. She said she used this wool in every rug she made. It literally added a common thread to all her rugs and made them even more meaningful.

I am doing the same with something from my mother's closet. This winter after my mother died, I took her green wool car coat. I used some of it to hook my initials into the rug I had been working on when I got the call that she had fallen. The coat still smells of her and I will use it in all my future rugs.

Naming Your Rug

Giving your rug a descriptive and thought-provoking title is an important means of telling a tale with a rug. It is also the simplest and most effective way of making a point with your rug. Calling a rug *Cat # 3* is fine, but it tells us little about the cat. The title is a chance to say what you want about your piece.

I sometimes write down a rug's story for a customer. It is a nice to have the story leave the studio with the mat and know that the story will be preserved. On the other hand, when I tell the story verbally and the new owner goes off with the mat, the story will change, and the mat will take on a life of its own. That's nice, too.

It's a lovely feeling to create something and have people respond emotionally to it. I have learned a lot about myself through hooking rugs, especially from the way people respond to them. So although I spend a lot of time hooking mats and putting stories into them, I do not guard the stories too closely. I like to see others respond to the rugs based on their own experiences, and I like to see the stories grow, just as they did when they were told around my parents' kitchen table long ago.

Élizabeth LeFort Hansford

In a community of rug hookers, one becomes a legend

I began hooking rugs quite a few years ago. I was enthusiastic, curious, and wanted to learn all I could about my new craft. For years as I traveled around the Maritime Provinces of Canada, I had seen the finely crafted floral coasters, chair pads, and rugs from the community of Chéticamp, Nova Scotia. And even though I lived in northern Nova Scotia, a six-hour drive from Chéticamp, something inside lured me to the place.

In many other areas around the Atlantic Provinces, the fiber art of rug hooking has virtually disappeared. Yet Chéticamp has somehow built an industry around rug hooking, and I found myself incredibly intrigued by this notion. So when I finally hopped in my car on a trip to satisfy my curiosity, I had no idea what kind of mysteries I would discover. Once in Chéticamp, I found my way to Les Trois Pignons and the work of Élizabeth LeFort Hansford.

Chéticamp

On this visit I spent the day perusing the shops of Chéticamp, even buying myself one of their famous rug hooking frames. Heading out of town driving along Cape Breton's spectacular coastal highway, I spotted a cheerfully painted building, sporting the red, white, and blue colors of the Acadian Flag. We stopped at what we later learned was Les Trois Pignons, or the Acadian Cultural Center, to learn a little more about where we were visiting. Once inside, we discovered that one of the galleries was completely devoted to the work of one rug hooker, Chéticamp resident Élizabeth LeFort Hansford.

Nature Scene, *25.6" x 34.4", two-ply wool on burlap. Hooked by Élizabeth Lefort, Chéticamp, Nova Scotia, Canada, 1981.*

Left: **Resurrection**, *9.9' x 8.25', two-ply wool on burlap. Hooked by Élizabeth Lefort, Chéticamp, Nova Scotia, Canada, 1963. Right:* **Jesus the Adolescent**, *4' x 3', two-ply wool on burlap. Hooked by Élizabeth Lefort, Chéticamp, Nova Scotia, Canada, 1963.*

It was impossible not to be astonished with the huge tapestry-like pieces that adorned the walls of the gallery. I remember standing there, looking at the fine work on the walls and realizing that with my new craft the possibilities were infinite. Ever since that moment, I have had great respect for the work of Élizabeth and for the potential of the art of rug hooking. She is both a skilled craftsperson and an artist.

An Artist's Beginnings

Élizabeth LeFort, one of Chéticamp's most famous daughters, was born in 1914, the child of Placide and Evangeline LeFort. She learned to hook rugs as a young girl from her mother. Initially, she worked with traditional patterns. Around the age of 27, however, she began to create her own designs, and she also became skilled as a dyer. In 1940,

she created her first design adaptation of a Christmas card, a barnyard pattern, using 28 shades of brown. She enjoyed this design and hooked it several times, one of which is in the collection of the gallery at the cultural center.

Élizabeth credits much of her success to Kenneth Hansford, a businessman from Toronto, who happened to stop at her door one rainy day. In an article in the *Family Herald* in 1961, she states that without his interest she would not have pursued rug hooking as an art, but as a craft, selling rugs to tourists.

Kenneth bought his first rug from Élizabeth, the same barnyard scene, for $45 and turned around and sold it for $200, later sharing the extra profit with Élizabeth. Knowing that he had stumbled upon someone of great talent, he bought all the rugs Élizabeth had and asked to purchase all the ones she made in the future. In 1951, he opened the Paul Pix Shop, selling handicrafts and souvenirs on a piece of land that he had purchased in Margaree Harbour. He was well aware of the potential of both Élizabeth and of Cape Breton as a tourist destination.

For many years, Élizabeth worked in Kenneth's shop for $50 a week. She had a fine studio there where she was able to hook all day long and demonstrate rug hooking to those who stopped by to visit. As her manager, Kenneth built a gallery to hang her rugs and gave her a great deal of direction in her career. He helped her publicize her work, chose designs for her to hook, and saw that she received proper attention for her work.

Élizabeth's Work Receives Recognition

One of the art forms that Kenneth encouraged Élizabeth to experiment with was portraiture. He felt that with her exceptional talent, she could create amazing portraits in wool. In 1955 she completed a portrait of the then-current president of the United States, Dwight D. Eisenhower. She struggled with this portrait, beginning it several times, but was completely satisfied with the final rug.

Seeing the finished work, Kenneth lobbied to have himself and Élizabeth invited to the White House, where they could present the portrait to the President, which they did in 1957. Later in a letter, President Eisenhower wrote to Élizabeth that he was "keenly interested in the unusual effects that you are able to create through the medium of hand hooking in wool yarn" (*Arizona Register*, Dec. 8, 1961).

In 1959, Élizabeth presented Queen Elizabeth with a portrait of herself during the queen's visit to Canada. She told the Queen that it took her only 11 days to create the piece using 50 different shades of yarn. The Queen quickly responded, "Eleven days of work, but no doubt a lifetime of experience"(*The Family Herald*, March 1961). The Queen quickly arranged to have the portrait shipped to her yacht in Halifax, and it has been hanging in Buckingham Palace ever since.

After these successful attempts at portraiture, Élizabeth went on to hook many other famous personalities. Her skill at turning strips of hand-dyed wool yarn, spun from Cape Breton sheep, into the famous faces of the 1950s and '60s

---

First Astronauts, 17.2" x 21.2" each, two-ply wool on burlap. Hooked by Élizabeth Lefort, Chéticamp, Nova Scotia, Canada. (Astronauts pictured are Lt. Col. John H. Glenn, Virgil Grissom, Gordon Cooper, Walter Schirra, Scott Carpenter, Alan B. Shepard, and Donald Slayton.)

Chéticamp
and Cape Breton, Nova Scotia

Upon leaving Margaree Harbour and heading into Chéticamp last fall, I was reminded that simple is beautiful. Colorful houses sit on hillsides overlooking the Atlantic Ocean, dotting the still and peaceful countryside. Folk art carvers, Cape Island fishing boats, lobster pots, fish and chips, and fiddlers at the local tavern on a Saturday afternoon are what Chéticamp seems to be all about.

If you venture into one of the many "boutiques" or souvenir shops along the way, however, you will see that rug hooking in this tiny French Catholic community of 3,500 may be as precious as the ocean's resources to the economic lifeblood of the village. Hooking began in Chéticamp the same way it did along the eastern seaboard of the United States, with women hooking rags onto burlap sacks. The shops are filled with hooked rugs, from coasters to large floor rugs. The rugs generally feature floral or bird motifs, but other subjects of community life, such as fishing scenes, can easily be found. The rugs are generally created from patterns on burlap, and hooked with fine yarn that is dyed by the maker. Many women in the community work all winter to create the mats that are sold in these shops, as well as in other shops across North America.

In the 1920s, Lillian Burke, an artist from New York, visited the area on an invitation from the daughter of the great inventor, Alexander Graham Bell, who lived in nearby Baddeck. Lillian had a profound influence on rug making in the area and helped the women develop their rugs into works that could be profitable in the United States. This was a great step for the community, as it helped bring the families of these craftswomen much-needed income.

These efforts, which began as handcrafts projects to put pocket money in the hands of women who needed it, continues to grow today, 75 years later. Not only can you find rugs in Chéticamp, but many of the boutiques also sell kits that come with a small hook that, even today, is fashioned by filing down a nail. ∎

allowed her to develop an international reputation as a master artist. Some of the images she painted in wool included President Johnson, Jacqueline Kennedy, Canadian Prime Minister John Diefenbaker, Lord Beaverbrook, Prince Charles, and the first seven American astronauts.

Religious Influences

Having grown up in Chéticamp, which has a strong Acadian French Catholic community, religion and church heavily influenced Élizabeth's work. She hooked portraits of both Pope Pius XII and Pope John XXIII. An Apostolic Delegate later presented the portrait to Pope Pius XII, and the rug now hangs in the Vatican Art Gallery.

Élizabeth also created a body of work reflecting the life of Jesus Christ as a child, adolescent, and adult. She reproduced the works of other famous religious artists to create rugs such as *The Last Supper*, *Christ at Calvary*, and *The Resurrection*. She believes that her depiction of The Last Supper, based on the painting by Leonardo Da Vinci, is her best work. In creating this rug, which measures 8' x 4$\frac{1}{2}$', she used 154 shades of yarn. Her tapestry of *Christ at Calvary* was even more demanding, as it required 510 different colors covering 55 square feet.

History in Wool

Two of Élizabeth's most famous and largest works celebrate the histories of both the United States and Canada. The first, entitled *My Country, 'Tis of Thee*, is approximately 6' x 10'. Created from 1959 to 1960, it depicts all the American Presidents and the important events that mark their careers. These portraits surround a center medallion featuring the Presidential Seal and the Seal of the United States.

To celebrate Canada's centennial, she created a 66-square foot rug, using 416 shades of wool illustrating important events in Canadian history. Like its American counterpart, this rug features portraits of the Canadian Prime Ministers. It also has the provincial Coats of Arms of each province and is full of cultural significance that spans from the Atlantic to the Pacific. To complete this rug, Élizabeth pulled nearly two million loops over a seven-month period.

Crucifixion, *9.9' x 6.5', two-ply wool on burlap. Hooked by Élizabeth Lefort, Chéticamp, Nova Scotia, Canada, 1964.*

Canada's Confederation (Centennial), *10' x 6.5', two-ply wool on burlap. Hooked by Élizabeth Lefort, Chéticamp, Nova Scotia, Canada, 1967.*

As you leave behind the fishing boats in Chéticamp, keep your eyes open for Les Trois Pignons, the Acadian Cultural Center, of which the LeFort Gallery is just a small part. La Société Saint Pierre, a group devoted to preserving Acadian Heritage, built this center. The center was constructed in an 18th century French Architectural Style similar to that used during the first settlement of Chéticamp. It has just undergone extensive renovations, and in addition to the LeFort Gallery, the center exhibits the works of other Chéticamp rug hookers, a fine collection of antiques, and an extensive library and historical archive. You can find out more at *www.lestroispignons.com*. ■

A Unique Style

Élizabeth's rugs are often described as tapestries because of the fineness of the work. Standing in front of them, particularly the larger murals at Les Trois Pignons, you marvel at her technical and artistic ability, and her sheer willpower to begin and finish such monumental pieces. She is clearly a hard worker, strong and purposeful in her pursuits. Oftentimes she would hook eight-hour shifts at The Paul Pix Shop, where she worked until 1974, when she moved her studio to a converted barn.

Élizabeth is also well known for the speed at which she can hook—55 loops in a minute, 3,300 in an hour, and 26,400 in a day. During the summers at her studio, she would demonstrate to tourists from all over the world. Some summers up to 150 bus tours would drop in to see the famous Chéticamp rug hooker in action.

She and Kenneth worked successfully together for many years and eventually married in 1967. In 1975, she was awarded an honorary doctorate from the University of Moncton, making her Dr. Élizabeth LeFort Hansford. In November 1981, Élizabeth and her husband struck an agreement with La Société Sainte Pierrre to take responsibility for over 20 of her wonderful works.

On August 2, 1983, Élizabeth was honored for all her talent and hard work with the opening of the Élizabeth LeFort Gallery. This is considered no small feat in a community where nearly everyone hooks rugs to sell to tourists in the summer. Her rugs stand out from many of the traditional Chéticamp rugs because of their size, their unlimited use of color, and their design. Today that gallery is visited by up to 400 tourists a day during the travel season.

A Life Well Lived

Élizabeth LeFort Hansford continues to hook rugs for a couple of hours every morning, except for Sundays, and still derives great pleasure from it. She is healthy and continues to live in her own home, where she helps out her older sister who uses a walker and is 96 years old. They rely on a local woman who comes in to help them out each morning. Élizabeth does not tell her own age, as she says, "It is nobody's business."

Élizabeth no longer works on huge tapestries but prefers instead to stick to smaller, simpler patterns and is currently working on a flowerpot design. She has had a long and productive life and has shone light on both her craft and her community. She has met many famous people, had many honors, and continues to hook rugs, no doubt like the rest of us, for the pleasure of it, the feel of the wool on our fingertips, and the peace and serenity that it offers.

Hooking Poppies

Poppies are forever

When I was fourteen I was walking down the hill above the fish plant in Jersey-side, Placentia Bay, with a friend. The water was below me. The sun was shining like it does on a day in late June. The water sparkled a deep blue and the evergreen hills rolled down to meet it. Boats were coming in and out from the wharf, fishermen were doing what fisherman do, hoisting and hauling from their boats to the wharf. A light wind was blowing off the water, and there, swaying in a overgrown yard by the side of the road, was a single red poppy, the first one I had ever seen. It was a new kind of red to me, poppy red. I went into the yard to have a look. I was as curious then as I am now.

Somehow I knew it was a poppy. Before that the only poppy I had ever seen was the little felt ones we wore for Armistice Day. On November 11 in Canada we all wear the poppy as a symbol of remembrance for those who fought in the war, or served in our armed forces. My Uncle Donald, a favorite of mine, fought in the British Navy during the Second World War. One day while we were on a drive he told me the story of being in a boat that was torpedoed off the coast of Africa, and how he

Modern Poppies, *10" x 18", 2013.*

Detail, with real poppy.

Left: **All Over Poppies**, *18" x 26", 2009.*

was floating around hanging on to a piece of the ship when he was picked up by a German boat and taken as a prisoner of war. There were over 400 men on that ship and only 18 survived. He was one of them. Uncle Don was a bachelor and worked on the high steel in New York City. He would come home every summer to Newfoundland, bringing gifts and spending money for the nieces and nephews. He was a kind man: when he wanted a chocolate bar he bought ten and gave nine away. So poppies remind me of him—of service and generosity and abundance.

I never really thought much about that poppy in Jerseyside—other than to occasionally remember it was beautiful—until years later when I decided it was time to hook poppies. Then that day flooded back into my memory. I can see myself, Deanne the teenager, who had no idea of ever becoming an artist, spotting that bit of beauty sparking in an overgrown yard. It makes me see that the artist was in me long before I ever knew it was there.

So the first step to hooking poppies is to find some and really look at them. Feel the petals. Aren't they silky and paper-like at the same time? Smell them. Is there much of a scent? Plant them in your garden. Watch that tiny back seed sprout and grow into the rigorous strong stalk that holds the delicate red petals. Watch the seedpod, how it turns from black to dark purple to navy in the light. How the stamens are so perfectly structured and how they recede as the petals fall and the green seedpod turns to caramel and then to grey. It will weather the winter unless you pick it off and shake it and watch the tiny black seeds that started it all fall out into the earth and it all begins again.

I honestly believe that the natural world is the place to start if you want to hook something. First, look at it in its natural state. Then you might take a picture of it, sketch it, or even pick it for your table. Whatever way you choose, you need to really look at it and examine it. I have planted poppies in my garden and get a dozen or so each year. They usually bloom near my birthday and I always go out and have a good look at them. The leaves are interesting—organic and ragged, long and narrow. If you want to hook a bloom, you need to know what the leaf looks like.

So think about why poppies inspire you. Why do you want to hook poppies? How do they inspire you? What do they remind you of? When was the first time you ever saw a poppy?

You also need to think of the design or context of your poppy rug. Are the poppies in a big field? Are they close-up? Are they in the foreground of a landscape? I have designed over fifty poppy rugs. Some are playful and the poppies are the focus; others just have poppies as the background. A background field of poppies, for example, is probably just areas of dark reds, with a few dots of red here and there to give the impression of a field. A large close up of a poppy would be very different; you will want to show more detail, the softness of the petal, the magnificence of the flower.

The Color of Poppies

For Brenda who works with me, poppies are coral. For me, poppies are only red. For you, though, they may come in another color. Years ago when I bought my house, pale pink poppies with sage-colored greenery kept popping up everywhere. That is another poppy variety. The truth is, you can also hook them in some imaginary color. I am going to explain what I do in reds and you can translate this information into any color.

— — — — — — — — — — — — — — — — — — — —

Poppies on the Edge, *30" x 20", 2008.*

Poppies and Houses, *17" x 11", 2008.*

CHOOSE YOUR MATERIALS FOR THE PETALS

Poppy petals are big and fall softly away from the stamen and center as they age a few days. It is this falling away that often makes them so interesting looking. You will be looking for materials that accentuate the smooth silky paper-like qualities of the petals.

Pick three shades of red wool cloth, one darker bluish red, one bright orangey red, and another pure red.

Pick two red yarns in similar shades to either of the three cloths. If one of the yarns has a silky sheen, that will highlight your petals.

Make sure none of the materials are heavily textured, plaids, or tweeds. Stick with smooth relatively solid colors, as poppies are smooth and silky. Use regular knitting yarns rather than fancy textured yarns.

I have suggested five colors for a rug of larger poppies that is about 24" by 24" and where the poppies are the main focus. If your poppies are smaller, you can use three colors. If they are larger, you might use seven to nine colors.

COLOR FOR THE DEEP DARK CENTERS

Those centers are so intriguing. The color is really dark, but yet not quite black. There is an element of purple and navy sheen to the darkness. Gather small scraps of black, navy, purple, or any plaids that are a combination of these colors. Use a bit of black velvet as a highlight. You will need some black yarn.

Hooking the Poppies

THE PETALS

First I outline the petals in purple or black to distinguish them from one another. I follow the outline drawn on the backing, but I make sure that my line is a little wonky, going inside and outside the lines that are drawn on the backing so the poppy will have loose soft edges. I also skip lots of holes, often choosing to outline in a number six so that it is not stiff.

Then I take each of my red fabrics and cut some of each in #6 and #8 widths. I will then take a

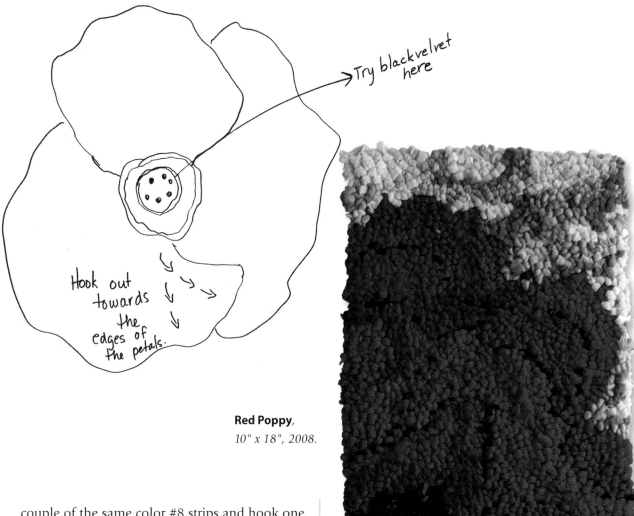

Try black velvet here

Hook out towards the edges of the petals.

Red Poppy,
10" x 18", 2008.

couple of the same color #8 strips and hook one of them—starting at the center and working out towards the edge of the petals. As I get to the edge of the petals, I make the line wider and thicker so that the shape looks like an irregular triangle. I make sure that I hook rather loosely and that my lines are not straight but irregular. I will take this same color and move it around the poppy sometimes in five or six places, using #6 and #8 cuts as if they were one. I normally work one flower at a time so that I can make each one unique, but I will work on several petals of the same flower. I will then start working in the second and third fabric in the same fashion, sometimes joining them with the first fabric. This will create oddly shaped areas that you can then fill in with the two yarns as you complete each petal. Occasionally I have been known to tuck in some red velvet, just a strip or three—not very much—to give an interesting focal point on my petals.

THE CENTERS

Take a strip of black velvet and hook a circle towards the center of center. Then take a tweed or plaid and hook tiny dots, pulling an end, a loop, and an end. I do this in a circle inside or outside the velvet circle. Either will work. You can then fill in with a circular motion, but not in complete circles, with your remaining dark colors. The dots will look a bit like the stamen, and the circle of velvet will make the center look rich and deep.

The center of the poppy is very interesting. You do not want to hook it round and round in circles;

rather, try to approximate what it really looks like. Create some interest and depth. You are using wool, so you cannot make it look perfect, but you can make it interesting, which I think is even better.

In Conclusion

All of the tips and thoughts in this article can be used to create any color poppies. You can use the tips to hook a single flower or a foreground field of poppies.

My best advice is always to experiment with color and texture and to hook several different poppy rugs. I suggest that before starting on a large project of poppies, you might want to complete four to six small projects or studies. These rugs themselves will be beautiful, but the real beauty of them is that you will learn so much from them,

both as you make the rug and as you later look at the completed rug.

Rug hooking is a learning process because every subject we choose requires a different set of skills to pull off the idea and turn it into a lovely rug. To get good at hooking a certain subject matter you need to hook it more than once; every time you hook it, you'll get a little closer to that beautiful idea you have in mind.

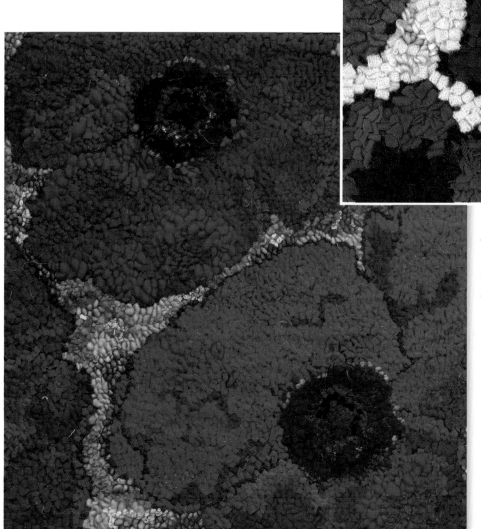

Above: **Poppy on Yellow**, *detail.*

Left: **Port Greville Poppies**, *24" x 24", 2012.*

Capturing the Essence

The art of hooking primitive people

It is impossible to know what moments will stay with us as we journey through our days. Long before I ever thought about hooking a rug, I was in a first-year anthropology class discussing primitive societies. My grizzly-bearded professor stood at the front of the class and told us that ". . . even the most primitive of societies is complex . . . it is a set of complex ideas that keeps that society working." The professor scoffed at people who simplified the idea of primitive. Little did I know that I would be reflecting on that discussion some 20 years later while thinking about making primitive hooked rugs.

A Primitive Way of Thinking

Designing and understanding a primitive pattern involves trying to get across an idea in the simplest possible way. At the outset, the pattern may appear as simple as can be, but there are more layers to that design than meet the eye. You have to understand the use of color, fabrics, texture, and design as they interrelate to a primitive style.

Hooking primitive people is very much like writing a good poem—you have to select a few choice words to impart a powerful understanding. While

hooking, however, you need to get across your idea of a person, or a character, by hooking wide strips of wool cloth on backing. This basic explanation sounds primitive enough, but I assure you that it is not as simple as it sounds.

The Girl Who Went Away, *26" x 38", #6-,8-, and hand-cut wool on burlap. Designed and hooked by Deanne Fitzpatrick, Amherst, Nova Scotia, 2001.*

Giving Thanks for the Harvest, *60" in diameter, #6-, 8-, and hand-cut wool on burlap. Designed and hooked by Deanne Fitzpatrick, Amherst, Nova Scotia, 1999.*

Remembering the Character

I have been hooking primitive people for over 10 years. Initially, they were just details in my mats, but as time went on they became the focus of my rugs. I first got really interested in them when I completed rugs of my childhood: one, a portrait of our next-door neighbor, an old man who threw fish guts on his garden for fertilizer, and the other, a picture of my Aunt Mary who was always kind to me.

Due to their primitive nature, these rugs were not portraits of these people, but rather a reflection of my memory of them. When you hook primitively, creating a portrait that reflects the fine features of the face is impossible. It is possible, however, to reflect the character of the person you are trying to create.

Last spring I presented a solo exhibit of my work at the Acadia University Art Gallery in Wolfville, Nova Scotia. This show was organized over a year beforehand, and I felt that it was important to create a body of work that hung together well and made a statement about something I believed in. I decided to hook a series of primitive portraits of people, which I called *The Common Soul*.

My creative intent was to show that whether rich or poor, we are all alike in so many ways. As my father (and probably your father) said, "We all put on our pants one leg at a time." To get ready for that show, I pulled out a few rugs of people that I had hooked over the years and saved, and then I spent the winter creating rugs that were either portraits of people I knew, or characters in stories

Dressing Them Up

Choosing what your people will wear is one of the things I enjoy most about hooking people. In primitive hooking this is where you really get to show who a person is. A uniform, rubber boots, an apron, or a hat can sometimes define who a person is in a primitive rug. When hooking clothing, you have no need to stick to solid colors. You can make it striped, floral, plaid, or patterned. I make a dress floral by hooking up two loops of a pretty floral color, such as mauve. Then right beside it, I will hook up a little loop of green. I then fill in the background with a lighter shade, such as pale yellow or cream. Stripes can be created by alternating colors as you hook. Plaids can be created by hooking a grid on the article of clothing in one color and filling it in with a contrasting color.

When I hook florals, stripes, or plaids, I often show folds in the fabric by hooking short curved lines of black that are about one-third the size or less of the article of clothing. These black lines show movement and flow. When I am hooking something in a solid shade, I often use several colors very close together to show this flow of movement.

As you hook clothing, be sure to focus on the details. Show the shape of a person in their clothes. Highlight a pocket, buttonholes, belts, and folds in the fabric. These little things give the rug dimension and make it interesting. You can add adornment to clothing such as a special button at the neck of a blouse, or a bit of jewelry, either by hooking these things in, or by attaching a special antique button. I have found that attaching things to rugs looks best when the items are subtle and small.

The importance of details cannot be overstated. At the same time it is important not to become more detailed that you can handle with a #6 or #8 cut. I have been known to cut a strip of #8 down the middle so that I could put a flower in a woman's hair. A small black line on the chest can show if a woman is buxom or lean. A ring on the finger, a feather in the band of a man's hat, or a bit of pink lipstick may only entail hooking up four or five loops of cloth, but they can make the rug sing and speak volumes about a person. ∎

I remembered. Doing this led me to think a lot about what is important in hooking people.

Getting Down to the Basics

When creating a primitive hooked portrait, you should reflect on exactly what it is you want to portray. The process is akin to becoming reacquainted with an old friend. Think about their features—what is the most prominent thing you remember? Reflect on their actions and hand movements. Did they hold their head with a certain tilt? How do they lay their hands on the table? For instance, my father held a cigarette loosely between his forefingers and held his arm across his belly. My mother held her handbag with both her hands right in front of her, and she always wore a patterned bandana. These simple gestures capture the essence of my parents' appearance.

Clothing is another important aspect that can tell you much about a person's character. Clothes give us information about a person's role in life, their work, and their value.

A rug hooker has to respect the medium or style they have chosen and do the best they can with that style, or they will frustrate themselves to no end. This is especially true when hooking in a primitive style. When primitive hooking with wide cuts of cloth of #6, #8, or higher, you should aim to simply show a person's essence by focusing on illustrating the most important features that describe them. This inspiration comes from reflection, but it also never hurts to be handy with a sketchpad.

Above: **Coming Home from Bingo**, *36" x 36", #6-, 8-, and hand-cut wool on burlap. Designed and hooked by Deanne Fitzpatrick, Amherst, Nova Scotia, 2001.*

Left: **Love and Forgiveness**, *30" x 70", #6-, 8-, and hand-cut wool on burlap. Designed and hooked by Deanne Fitzpatrick, Amherst, Nova Scotia, 2001.*

Sketching

Sketching is often an underrated tool in rug hooking. It seems to be a chore to many, especially those who believe they cannot draw. People generally do not carry around a sketchbook like they do their frame or their cutter. If you want to create original designs, however, it's a great way to get started. Drawing the person that you want to hook is an essential exercise because it will trigger your visual memory of the person. You may not be lucky enough to get it right the first time, so a series of sketches often does the trick.

When finished, look over the sketches and pick out the elements that look right to you. The time

Common Souls, *14" x 68" each, #6- and #8-cut wool on burlap. Designed and hooked by Deanne Fitzpatrick, Amherst, Nova Scotia, 1999.*

spent sketching is time spent thinking about the person you want to depict. The more time you devote to it, the better you will understand your subject, and your rug hooking will make a stronger statement.

Photographs

Photographs are also helpful in creating your concepts of primitive people, but keep them in the album for now. I suggest that you sketch first to sort out your own ideas and go through photographs second, keeping your goal in mind to find a picture that really sums a person up. I do not usually use photographs, but they can be helpful to accurately reflect what a person looks like at a given period in their life. They can also serve to jog the memory.

Photos can also be a hindrance, however. We sometimes feel we have to depict everything that is in the photograph just as adequately as the photograph does. This is an impossible task, as we must remember that photography is a different medium. If you are trying to create a primitive portrait by looking at an old or new picture, the first thing you will need to do is start eliminating the peripheral material. If you try to pack too much into your rug, the person will not stand out. It is important to select just the right picture, the one that captures the person as you see them or believe them to be. You can then go back to the sketchbook, using the photograph as a tool to define your pattern.

Final Thoughts

The context of the person in the mat is important. If they are the central figure, they need to be large and in the foreground. In a rug called *The Girl Who Went Away*, I put the red-headed girl in the foreground holding her bright red suitcase to show

Grace, Mercy, and Peace, *36" x 36", #6-, 8-, and hand-cut wool on burlap. Designed and hooked by Deanne Fitzpatrick, Amherst, Nova Scotia, 2001.*

Above: **The Virtuous Wife**, *4' x 5', #6-, 8-, and hand-cut wool on burlap. Designed and hooked by Deanne Fitzpatrick, Amherst, Nova Scotia, 2000.*

Left: **The Pickers**, *4' x 5', #6-, 8-, and hand-cut wool on burlap. Designed and hooked by Deanne Fitzpatrick, Amherst, Nova Scotia, 2000.*

Creating Primitive Faces

Hooking the face is seen as the most threatening part of hooking primitive people. I try to keep this process simple, as I have found that when I spend too much time on the details of a person's face, it can take on a cartoon-like quality, making the rug feel more like a spoof than a piece of art. If you hook with finer cuts, you could use them in the face if it was important for you to show some details. I choose not to because I am looking for a primitive effect in the whole rug. I prefer the way that it looks, and the feeling that it evokes.

For a large face, say one that is 4" x 6", I will generally use four to six shades of light tan or camel. For a smaller face I will use two or three shades. I cut some in #6 cuts and some in #8 cuts, as this will add a textural quality that can show a bit of movement in the face.

Generally, I will take the shades that stand out a bit—perhaps it is darker, or lighter, or has tweed or some texture to it— and set these shades off to the side. I will use these sparingly, perhaps to shape a hollow for the cheek or a crook in the face for the nose. Usually these are hooked in one thick line with two lines in a few places to accentuate it. I then choose a second shade, often lighter, to show the forehead and cheeks. With the other shades I fill the face in randomly.

If there are several people in one rug, I usually add an extra shade, or change around the way I use the shades for each person, so that each face has its own unique look. Adding pale peach, cream, chocolate browns, medium browns, and different shades of tans and other natural colors can change the race and the coloring of the people you are hooking. I sometimes like a bit of pale pink on the lips or the cheeks to show someone whom always wore a bit of makeup.

Generally, I look for good skirt-weight wools, camel hair coats, and light tan tweeds rather than paler flesh tones of wool. I use those for accents and details.

The faces are then framed by hair, for which I generally use natural sheep's wool. I will dye this wool based on individual hair color or choose gray wool for an older person's hair. The natural sheep wool takes the dyes easily. One of the best batches of natural sheep's wool I ever had was dyed with walnut hulls on the back of a wood stove. These came out every shade of brown and auburn you could imagine. Rusty red, gold, browns, tans, and black are all useful for hair. You could pull the wool into strands, and hook the strands as if they were regular cut cloth. The effect will be fluffy and higher than the rest of the rug, as hair often is. It can be trimmed up and sculpted with scissors to flatten it out or shape it. ▪

that she was leaving. In the background were a gold farmhouse, a line of laundry, and a woman holding a laundry basket. These elements lead to a lot of discussion. Where was she going? Who was left behind? The context that the girl was placed in is an important part of the story, but it should not overtake the portrait.

I sometimes use a nice wide border to surround the portrait to put in symbols of the people or things that remind me of them. Other times I use the border as purely decorative, a chance to add color and fauna to the rug.

You can also put something in a person's hand to tell a bit more about them. Did they often bring you bread? Work in the garden? Like to fish? What inanimate object could they be holding that would further describe them?

As always when I hook, I spend half the time following rules (only the ones I have created for myself), and I spend half the time breaking them and experimenting with new ideas. Remember that you are hooking your vision of a particular person in a primitive style. If you want an exact replica of the person, there are much better mediums available to you than rug hooking, and of course, there are already plenty of photographs of them in the drawer.

Letting Light In

The light paints the landscape. Every time I walk out my door it is different than the time before. You can never capture it the same way twice. That is the beauty of hooking the landscape—the light is always changing, so every time you approach it, the view is different. My landscape, or field rugs as I like to call them, started with a walk in the country. The beauty of walking the same few miles every day is that you see the same thing over and over again. Where's the beauty in that, you might say? Isn't boring? Well, it could be, I suppose, if it weren't for the light—if it weren't for the details. When you walk the same road and see the same landscape day after day, you begin to watch it closely and notice the small things.

A routine helps you see beauty in the smallest of things. When you discover that the sun paints the landscape with its own brush depending on where it is, you learn that every time you look at the land around you it will be slightly different. No two moments are ever the same. The beauty of this is that you are given a lot of leeway to be imaginative and to create using your own sense of color. The variations are endless, and all are possible.

You need to be a student of the landscape you want to recreate. Look at it closely, admire it, study it and capture it. When you walk away from it,

Summer Bloom, *19" x 7", 2016.*

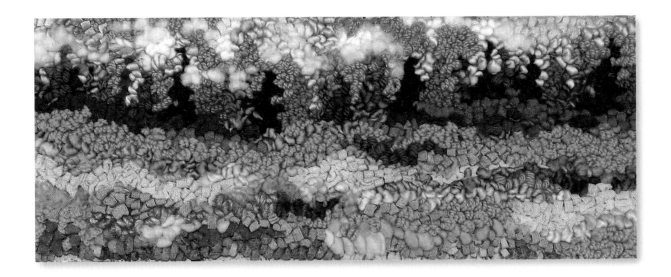

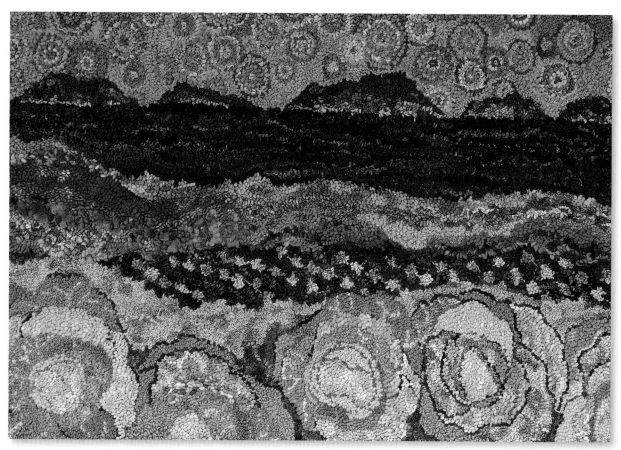

Cabbages on Coast, *60" x 54", 2013.*

you could close your eyes and try to recreate it in your mind. Remember the colors and the lines, the shapes of the trees, the texture of the field. Your rug starts in your mind as an inspiration. So the first and most important step to creating great landscape rugs is to study the world around you. Drink up the colors, and take in the texture of the fields, hills, and craggy rocks. Working from a picture is one thing, but getting to know the land with your own two eyes will lend a new dimension to what you can offer to your rugs.

Start to hook your mat based on your study of the landscape. There is no good design without inspiration. By the time you sit down to design the mat, you will have sketched it out and played with your ideas a little. Before you put the hook to the frame you will understand and know the character of the landscape you are trying to capture. There are many simple techniques that can help you create sweeping landscapes that romance the eye and are interesting to look at.

As you hook your landscape be sure to consider these factors:

The first thing you must decide is the subject of the landscape. Just what type of landscape do you want to create?

Once you choose the subject or place you want to recreate you will have to decide what the important elements are that need to be included. Pare it down to those elements that give you the feeling of the place. For example, in a large rambling farmscape, you might choose to put in the house, the two barns, the big elm tree, and the rose bushes. You might decide to leave out the battered chicken coop, and the broken down truck, depending of course on the feeling you want to create. You might decide just to have a corner of the house off in the distance.

One place can be captured in hundreds of different ways. How do you see it? If you want a quiet pastoral feeling, perhaps the truck and coop are out. If you want a lonesome feeling you might want to leave in some of the rundown elements.

You can also change things around, omitting power lines, or adding in a flower garden.

Remember: you want to create a beautiful mat and this may require a little adapting. The other important thing to remember is that a subject is not fixed. Remember to edit. Know what to leave out. Get rid of the objects that obscure the view, crowd it or throw off the composition. It is as simple as this: no one ever adds in the garbage box at the end of the rural lane. It just might not belong in the art work, even though it may belong in real life.

The same landscape can be done over and over again, in different lights, and by changing the elements of the picture. Think of how the Group of Seven painters went back to the same kind of landscapes again and again. They were in love with that landscape. Think of Emily Carr's relationship with the British Columbia forest. It captivated her.

Often artists are discouraged from looking at the same subject too closely. It is thought that they are not moving forward. I like to think that sometimes I am on a slow train ride in my work, and that extra time gives me a chance to look at one area really closely.

You can create a series or use a particular landscape as a theme in your work. This allows you to focus on different details and different feelings each time you approach it. It gets rid of the feeling that you have to do it exactly right the first time and can loosen you up a little. Subjects do not end because you hook them once. You can approach a landscape again and again, emphasizing different elements.

I love to play with the same subject matter, over and over again. I will often hook a landscape in different formats. I might sketch it out as a close up, a panoramic view, a horizontal view, a vertical, or a wide open view.

Play with the shape of your rugs. Think of squares, circles, or oddly shaped edges as possible formats for a landscape. In a close up, you might pick out a house or a tree and really focus in on the details of the landscape. The panoramic view shows a wide narrow slice of the landscape, allowing you to create sweeping fields and show a broad landscape. It is one of my favorite formats because so many different elements of the landscape can be shown in a single mat. A horizontal or long thin mat allows you to show distance well, as you can

----

Moon Over Country Road, *36" x 22", 2009.*

layer fields, hills, and houses—showing elements of the landscape that might be miles away. A wide-open format is usually a fat rectangle and allows you to show some expanse and some depth. It is a very traditional format and works well for many subjects. You can also create a series of rugs in the form of a diptych or triptych. I like to create series of squares of related landscapes that are not all necessarily a part of one larger image but separate images created in the same format: for example, four squares hung together.

Hook It the Way You See It

The way that you see the landscape you want to recreate will often determine the format, but you might have to play around with it to decide. There will be a natural instinct towards a certain shape or format. But remember that you have some choice here and can expand the horizon if you like. Sketching the landscape in different formats will get you thinking about your subject more clearly and help you know it better. It will make you consider the land, and that will be time well spent.

Once the format is decided, you will divide that format into the foreground, the middle ground, and the background. The foreground is the lead-in

Pines at the Lake, *44" x 32", 2013.*

to your landscape. In this area I often place a point of interest to draw the viewer into the mat, such as a bit of a fence, a bunch of bushes, or even the edge of a building. The middle ground of the mat is often the main part of the mat and holds many of the important elements of the subject. The background is the furthest away from the front of the mat and is the part that leads you to the sky.

Those are the main parts of traditional landscape composition. In creating a good composition for our rugs, we are struggling to create the very best arrangement of all the important elements of the landscape. You will need to carefully consider balance as you place these elements. You want the rug to feel as if there is balance between the elements as well as between the colors and textures you have chosen.

Wool for the Landscape

Choosing the wool for your landscape rug is important. You need a big stash to hook good landscapes because of the nature of showing light upon the land. You need many shades of each color so that you can vary them in the landscape.

If your hands are nimble and the wool cupboard is well stocked, you can make a little magic, a little moonlight, or sail the seven seas.

It is all about texture in these landscape mats. You want to take on texture, and begin to feel natural and comfortable working with it. Sylvia MacDonald, a well-known Nova Scotia rug hooking teacher, would say, "You are painting with wool."

Textures are what makes my landscape rugs interesting to look at and interesting to hook. They allow you to add dimension to the landscape. Your stash of wool should include Shetland sweaters, angora sweaters, fancy yarns, mohair, natural sheep's wool dyed and undyed, thready fabrics, bouclé, carded sheep's wool, tweeds, and plaids, silk yarns, eyelash yarns, merino wool, wool jersey.

Be fearless. Scour secondhand stores, thrift shops, find unusual fabrics. As long as you enjoy hooking with it, it is worth playing with. There is nothing better than finding a great angora sweater or a green jersey dress for your wool cupboard, but trying new and other interesting fabrics could lead you to something even better. You will need a wide variety of shades, particularly of greens, golds, and blues. I also like rusts, ambers, wines, teals, and mauves in my field rugs.

The colors you need depend on the season you are depicting. It would be great if you could send someone out with a list of what you need but it does not work like that. A great stash of wool is a work in progress, and you need to keep picking up those fancy bits and pieces to keep your cupboard interesting and inspirational. It is the gathering together of many types of wool from so many different places that makes our work charming. It is the old metaphor of a weaving together the different bits of a life: a scarf from here, a ball of yarn you picked up somewhere, the old coat of your sisters. A wide selection of texture and color is essential. You will discover that there are as many colors in nature as one can imagine and that a wide range of both color and texture will be important. Remember that exactly the same color in three different textures will act like three different wools in your mat. I love to use yellow cloth, yellow silk, and perhaps yellow merino yarn as if it were one color for an area of a field, because it

gives dimension, making the field feel like it has some movement.

How I Hook Landscapes

When I hook these landscapes or field rugs, I like to hook large areas in one tone of the same color. I lay out large areas of colored wool cut up for easy access. It is tempting to keep changing colors every two or three strips but this would be a big mistake. This might give you confetti or hit and miss look to your rug which will detract from the landscape. You do not want your rug to be spotty. You want large areas of color to show large expanses of land. A quick color change is what is needed for close-ups and small details. Create areas of similar colors that distinguish one pasture from another. You could use a dark line of a contrasting color to separate one field from another but it is not essential. One field can be separated from another just by contrasting the colors of the fields. For example, you might put gold up against khaki green; you'll clearly be able to see that there is a transition in this area of the mat.

Directional hooking is one of the techniques I use. If I want to show that the wind is blowing I will hook with a slant in the direction of the wind. If the pasture is a big rounded hill, I will hook in big rounded strokes. I have spent many hours over the years studying landscape painting to see what I can learn from the painters' strokes—there is much to be learned and the techniques borrowed from oil painters can easily be translated to rug hooking. I encourage you to pore over the books of your favorite painters or stand before them in galleries and study the way they have moved their paintbrush to get a desired effect. It is helpful.

Sky, sea, rivers, ponds, trees, plants, bushes, grass, flowers, fences, and buildings are the most important parts of the landscape.

When I hook the sky, I first think about what *kind* of day it is. I also consider what time of day it is. If it is a bright sunny day, I need one set of blues. If it is the evening light, I need a whole other set of colors, perhaps some gray-blues and mauves. If a storm is approaching, I need to get out some grays. For a bright day, I gather several light baby blues

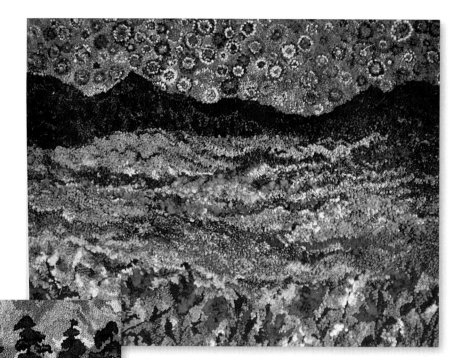

Above: **Hundred Acres**, *60" x 52", 2011.*

Left: **Seven Trees**, *72" x 65", 2014.*

together and some natural sheep's wool for clouds. I hook the clouds first and add in the blues after. I hook each of the blues in large fat areas like cumulus clouds themselves, working it up really close to the clouds of sheep's wool. This gives the effect of a large sunny day. If evening was approaching, I would be quick to add some mauves or even the palest yellow into the mix. I might hook the lower parts of the sky in long thinner areas rather than big cumulus areas. Sky contributes a lot to the overall feeling of the rug, and the colors you choose for it should relate to the rest of the colors you use in

the landscape. Remember there is a relationship between, sea, sky, and land. The colors of all of these are all affected by each other.

The sea is an exciting part of hooking the landscape. A stormy sea might require aquas, deep blues, navy, and some deep blue greens. A calm sea might need four shades of nearly exactly the same deep blue. Tidal water might need to be a brown overdyed blue so that you can see the mud rising underneath the water. Pendleton shirts of dark blue and aqua plaid make great water, but I always add something extra, a few different wools for interest. I do not like to hook a plaid as the only wool for any important element of the landscape because it looks as if that is just what I did. I mix it up to make it interesting. This draws the viewer in to see just what is going on, after they have been first captivated by the overall image.

Plants and trees jump off my rugs when I hook them with natural sheep's wool. For trees, bushes, and plants I show the branches with a bit of dark brown or a deep wine. For the leaves, I will often hook dyed green sheep's wool very high to show a puffiness. When I use sheep's wool I often pull the loops up to an inch high. When I pull the next loop, it pulls the last loop back down again. When I use sheep's wool I take a puffy piece and sort of hand card it into a loose strand, then hook it gently. The thinner and looser the strand, the further it will go. If it has a nice curly end I will sometimes leave that end up and not trim it off, so that it has a dramatic windblown effect.

Flowers and flower gardens are also easy to recreate with dyed sheep's wool and fancy variegated yarns, hooked up with a little green beside it. Take several colors of sheep's wool and keep changing the color, hooking small area of one color, and poking a little green in beside it. I like to hook the sheep's wool in colorful squiggly vertical lines, as these approximate tall standing flowers like hollyhocks and delphinium. Think of the shapes of the flowers you want to approximate and try to give the impression of their shape with the wool. Once you step back from your hooking, you little mess will transform itself from a few bits of woolies into a country garden.

I taught a one-day workshop on using wools this way and it was amazing what came up in people's gardens. Some added a little grey tweed and formed rock gardens. Others hooked in tiny bits of silk ribbon, almost as flecks, and showed delicate low ground covers. The more you experiment the more you will learn. Remember that flowers create a point of interest, and you should distribute the color in a way that works for the overall mat. Think about where you add these dramatic flourishes, as they have a lot of impact.

These field rugs are impressionistic. When you hook a building you can give it a feeling of being in the distance by bringing the land up to meet it rather than squaring off the bottom of the house. Avoid using textured wools in the buildings, as this will confuse the buildings with the landscape. Let the building recede by using plain woolens in solid colors. I generally use subtle colors for the houses in these rugs because, though I sometimes want to use a building as a point of interest or to show some life, I do not want it to be the focal point of the rug. I want people to be carried over that field like they are on a magic carpet. Often in my field rugs, the houses will be cream or grey so that they stand out from the landscape but do not overpower it.

If your landscape rug is going to be interesting, then your stash of wool needs to be just as interesting. You must be a student of the landscape you want to create. Know it and watch it and this will come through in your rugs.

Landscapes All Around Us

All good rugs—all good art in fact—follow basic design principles that are centered around composition, balance, and format. Make sure your landscape design incorporates these elements of composition. Do not be afraid to experiment. These rugs require texture as it adds the dimension they need.

Hook in broad sweeping areas, thinking about the shape of the area you are hooking as an acre or two of land. I use nice curved lines for hills, contrasting this when I hook spruce trees with small dashes of dark colors hooked across in zigzag fashion. The direction that you hook in will be seen in the finished rug and is part of the beauty.

As you hook landscapes, relax your hands and mind as if you were going for a gentle walk on the land itself, and your rug will tell the tale of your journey. I think of each field rug as if it is a piece of land of my own where I am creating a massive garden.

A man who lives up the road from me farms a few fields, and one year he filled it with a mauve timothy that blew in the wind. Another year it was filled with sunflowers. These fields became big and beautiful mounds of color. There seemed to be more beauty than one field could possibly hold.

Think of the space you have to hook this way: Every loop you hook is like planting a seed in a field. As you hook, it multiplies, and your linen or burlap is filled with a field of color. Plant wildly and watch the landscape take shape around you. It is your rug, your landscape to create. Use your hands to transform that little piece of backing into something fabulous in itself, a hooked rug.

Design 101

Using templates to create your own rug

How many times have we heard the old saying, "What goes around, comes around?" As with most old sayings there is a ring of truth to it. Templates have long been a popular tool of the craftsperson, and their time has come around again. They have long been used for making rugs, quilts, and other handcrafts. Templates act as simple cutouts, or stencils, and are used to trace a design of your own making onto the backing of your choice. Many people are surprised by the concept of drawing a pattern or design freehand on burlap. They have grown up with the idea that they cannot draw. Templates allow the freedom to design rugs without knowing how to draw.

Discovering Templates

I have always been enchanted with the old tools of my trade. I love old hooks made with a nail and chunk of wood, the patina on antique rug frames,

and the excitement of finding an old Bluenose pattern. A few years ago I went to the Canadian Museum of Civilization's show of hooked rugs and was delighted to see that they had a room dedicated to these tools. One of the focal points was a collection of brown paper templates that had been part of a rug hooker's tool collection in Quebec. They were creased and worn but still useable. Years ago, a rug hooker's templates were a valuable tool as they enabled her to create unique designs. They were shared with relatives, friends, and neighbors so that they, too, could recreate similar designs.

Once I was visiting a 90-year-old woman who had moved to a small apartment from her big country farmhouse. Upon hearing I hooked rugs, she went to a trunk where she kept the treasures

----

Three Sheep and Three Barns, *6"x 29", #6- and #8-cut wool on burlap. Designed and hooked by Deanne Fitzpatrick, Nova Scotia, Canada, 2003.*

House and sheep template. This design is free for individual or personal use only.

Below: Sheep template.

she could not part with when she gave up house-keeping. In the old black trunk were some fine linens, a quilt, an antique blue willow platter, and her templates for making mats. She told me that she quit mat hooking long ago but kept the patterns just in case. The templates were patterns of scrolls, roses, and flowers, simply drawn on butcher's paper and old brown paper bags. They were folded, creased and worn, and looked their age. They were among the few precious things saved from a lifetime of collecting. That visit showed me the importance of templates, both in their useful-ness and in their personal meaning to the owner.

Templates of the Past

At the turn of the century, and perhaps even before, women carefully saved the brown paper wrapping from store-bought goods to make templates for their mats. In those days, women would copy the design from a favorite china cup or trace the rose from the stamped pattern they bought from the door-to-door peddler. They would use them time and time again in different ways, creating their own mats to warm the parlor or greet the back-door visitors. Templates are a time-honored tradition

Hit and Miss Sheep, *6" x 8", #6- and #8-cut wool on blank. Designed and hooked by Deanne Fitzpatrick, Nova Scotia, 2003.*

and as much a part of rug hooking as the "stamped back" patterns drawn or stenciled onto burlap.

Today you can create templates by using copyright free designs and clip-art booklets, by drawing a simple design yourself, or by having someone draw one for you.

Using the Templates

Templates are a chance for any rug hooker to experiment with design and play with a new idea. A fun activity for a rug hooking group would be to have each member take a set of two or three identical templates, such as the sheep and house used here, and work individually to create and hook a small design. The variety would be sure to surprise all members of the group. Even though we might work from identical templates, we will naturally put our own spin on each design.

The simplest method of using the templates is to photocopy them onto card stock, cut them out, and trace them onto the preferred backing to create an unique stamped pattern. They can also be copied onto tracing fabric or paper, clear plastic

overheads, or even, as in the old days, a brown paper bag. As these templates are used, please feel free to mix them with other templates, designs, and patterns to create your own personal creations.

The designs can be enlarged to make a larger rug. Use the enlarged sheep and smaller sheep or house together in the same mat to show perspective, with the larger design in the foreground. The templates can also be adapted by tracing them out at an angle, or in reverse, so that the sheep are facing in different directions.

The house can be altered by adding or removing windows, or by putting in a door. Lay the templates on your backing and trace them to create one of the designs shown, or create your own. Draw a line in the foreground portion of the house to approximate a hill or field in front of the house.

To create your own design, begin by laying the templates directly on the burlap, moving them around and configuring different designs before beginning to trace the templates. Another option is to take a large piece of paper and actually use the templates to trace a design on paper before starting to draw right on the burlap. This allows more time to experiment before committing yourself to a design. If you do draw directly on the burlap and it is not exactly the design wanted, the burlap can be turned over and started on the other side. Rug hooking is a forgiving craft and provides a second chance right at the start.

I have found that using red and black markers helps me distinguish between what is in the foreground and what is in the background when I am creating a pattern with templates.

Hooking the House and Sheep Designs

Even when I am using templates and creating a simple design, I often add a little texture. Most of the sheep in these designs are hooked with natural sheep wool. I have also used cream wool cloth. For sheep I like to pull the wool nice and high so that they stand out a little from the background. Try hooking one black sheep amongst the fluffy white ones.

Sheep in the Purple Flowers, *5" x 7", #6- and #8-cut wool. Designed and hooked by Deanne Fitzpatrick, Nova Scotia, Canada, 2003.*

Right: House template. This design is free for individual or personal use only.

A simple technique for hooking a realistic field of flowers is to hook the cloth in vertical lines that are not straight. Three or four greens of various shades are needed. Hook in several floral colors such as the four shades of purples used here. In the fields I have chosen various light to medium greens and mixed them together. The sheep's face and legs are hooked in black for the dramatic look of a Suffolk sheep. A little natural sheep wool dyed a pale blue was used to give a measure of dimension to the sky. Using #6- and #8-cut wool together in the rugs gives added proportion and texture to the project.

Feel free to vary the colors from those that I have chosen in order to make the mat your own.

Why Use a Template?

Designing is not an essential part of rug hooking because there are so many good designers selling wonderful patterns. Choosing stamped patterns and distinguishing them with your own beautiful selection of color is a perfectly gratifying way to spend your time. From time to time I still like to hook an old fashioned floral or hit and miss mat; the simplicity of the design is soothing. More and more I meet people who, though they rely mostly on patterns, would like to experiment with design a little bit. Templates are an answer for the beginner, as well as the experienced designer—a tool, a trick of the trade, something that can be pulled out of a hat now and again for a little entertainment.

Having Fun with Templates

- Look through a child's coloring book, free clip-art books, or newspaper and magazine ads to see what possibilities you can find for templates. Be sure to respect copyright law and the hard work of rug hooking designers by not lifting their ideas. Instead challenge yourself to create templates. Most likely ideas will begin to appear everywhere.
- Have a template swap in your rug-hooking group. Ask each member to come to the next meeting with a template design. Bring along some extra card stock so that you can copy and share the templates with each other.
- Challenge yourself to create as many designs imaginable with the sheep and house templates included here. How many different ways can they be arranged to create as many patterns as possible?
- Remember that color can completely change the look of a mat. Try hooking the sheep with a brown face in tea-dyed natural sheep's wool. Imagine how much more playful the house would be if it had a roof of hit and miss stripes.
- Use the templates as the design elements of a border in a larger floor mat, and hook the center of the rug in a swirl of color.
- Add some more templates to the sheep and house and use them together in the same design. Rug hookers traditionally collected templates as part of their stash. The more varieties of roses and scrolls they could collect, the grander their designs could become. ■

Big Boned Girls

The inspiration behind a series of mats

O ne night last winter I was going out to
a rug-hooking group, the Highland
Hookers, that meets on Tuesday night
in Amherst. I needed something small for my lap
frame and decided to make a small series of rugs
of women, each one an individual piece, featuring
one woman.

I wanted a project that I could hook on my grip-
per frame without having to move the burlap. I
wanted each piece to be easy to finish in a sitting
or two. I decided on a size of approximately 6^1/$_2$" x
13" to 14". The size would vary slightly depending
on the size and shape of each woman.

Initially I thought I would do a series of six or so,
but after I got started, I discovered that there were
so many interesting women around me, let alone
the women I could make up or imagine, that my
discovery had infinite possibilities.

I am fortunate to be able to make my living
through my art. I run a rug-hooking studio and
gallery in the downtown of Amherst, Nova Scotia.
For nearly 20 years I have sold my rugs, patterns,
and kits.

At first I was calling these small rugs "little
women," but the title just did not fit them. The

Big Boned Girls, A Series, *7" x 13", #6- and #8-cut
wool, fleece, and fancy yarns on burlap. Designed and
hooked by Deanne Fitzpatrick, Amherst, Nova Scotia,
2008. A series of big boned girls mats.*

women were more industrious, and there was nothing little about their personalities. Finally I settled on "big boned girls," as that was how my mother referred to me when I was younger. My series of big boned girls was born.

Observing Women

This winter I took a course on using creative arts for transformational learning to keep my life interesting. I wanted to find creative ways to teach rug hooking. There were 18 women sitting in a circle for five days learning about using art to teach ideas. It was a new experience for me to be the learner after years of being the teacher.

I kept my sketchbook out most of the time and found myself watching the women in the group. They were creative dressers: one woman liked to wear big thick socks with skirts, another had a penchant for simple feminine dresses, another liked long "hippie" skirts and scarves.

I would watch the women seated around me and sketch elements of their outfits. I noticed small things like the shape of their collars, the folds of their scarves, the type and placement of buttons, the patterns in their clothes. The color of the shoes, the hairstyle, the shape of the hat, the cut of the jacket, the length of the skirt—each element of style of clothing says something about the person

you are hooking. It is the little details that will make a small mat special.

You can gather ideas for these big boned girl mats from your friends, acquaintances, coworkers, or even strangers at the grocery store. You can use pictures or fashion catalogs or magazines to generate ideas for the clothing!

Hooking a Series

All the women in the small mats I designed are wearing dresses or skirts. My favorite styles are from the forties and fifties, but great designs can be found in every era. Personally, I enjoy wearing

skirts and dresses in the summer heat. I love the relaxed feel of a comfortable dress.

These big boned girl mats use up the small amounts of fabric and cut wools that have little use in larger projects. Here you can use up the last of a great piece of wool in a woman's blouse or skirt and really showcase the last of that beautiful fabric. I save all the leftover cut strips from my larger rugs in zip-closure bags. When I am working on my women series, I throw all the bits into a basket so I have a wealth of colors to work with as I create prints and patterns on their clothing. Even one or two strips of a beautiful colour can be a great embellishment on a woman's dress. In such a small rug, the very last strip of a yard of fabric can be the rug's defining element.

Getting Started

To start designing, you can create a template of a woman and keep changing the clothing and hairstyle. If you decide that you would like to hook some big boned girl rugs like I have, you might want to start with some of the following ideas:

- Begin by clipping from magazines and catalogs the styles of dresses that intrigue you. From those clippings start sketching. Notice the lines around the bust, waistline, and collar, for these are the details you will want to accentuate.

- Look through your photo albums and pull out the pictures of friends who are interesting dressers. Grab your pile of pictures and sit with your sketchbook for an evening and see what happens.
- Sit at a mall or other public place that gets lots of foot traffic and watch the people who walk by. Bring a sketchpad so you can quickly draw or jot down notes on the styles that catch your eye.

Designing Dresses

Once you decide upon a design and have put it on backing, you will want to go through your wool stash and pull out the bright and pretty colors for clothing. I always pull out some dark navy, wine, or black for outlining. I cut the outlining color in a #6, but it could be even finer. When I outline these little beauties, I really consider what needs to be defined and concentrate on that. I always outline what I want to highlight, but that may be different depending on the style of the dress.

For example in a dress with a cinched waist, the waist might get outlined. When I outline the form of the woman I often do it really lightly and skip lots of holes. I want definition but not an outline that is so dark and heavy that it overtakes the woman. You do not want the outline to be the main thing you see.

Often, if the woman has on a dress, I will pick a color for the main part of the dress and a contrasting accent color that I might use to show a collar or belt. For example, this always works when you use white upon a navy or royal blue accent. As another example, to create a floral print in the dress, I might hook one or two loops of pink in random spots all over the dress. I will then accent each of these with a tiny bit of bright green and fill in the main body of the dress with golds or yellows.

Using two colors very close together in value (i.e., two yellows or two reds) will always add flow to the clothing. Even when it is hooked randomly, it will appear as if light and shadow are falling upon the clothing. This simple secret adds a lot of drama to hooking clothing.

You can accentuate a dress with a tiny bit of sparkly fabric or fleece to act as a broach or a corsage. Sometimes you can sew on a tiny button,

or attach an earring if the rug calls for it. Be careful here. Because the mats are small, any bit of embellishment can end up being the focal point instead of the woman herself.

If it is winter and she is wearing a coat, try a bit of brown or white fleece on a collar to act as fur. I also use fleece at the trim on a hat. For that matter, you could even hook a whole coat as fur.

Duplicating Skin

For the areas of skin tone I generally use two tans, very close together in tone, and hook the face, hands and legs. Sometimes I use a darker tone for the legs because when women wear panty hose, they are often a darker tone. Though I have never hooked with panty hose, I believe that it would work well as the skin tone for these big boned girls.

So if you have trouble finding wool, the solution might be in the top drawer of your dresser.

Adding Hair

For hair, there is nothing better than a bit of natural fleece dyed in a hair color or left natural if your woman is older. Sometimes I like to use dark brown wool strips, which make the hair look straighter than it does with fleece. With these little mats I even get to play hairdresser, something else I did as a child.

Creating a Background

The backgrounds you hook on these little mats are the settings for the personalities that you are creating. Remember this as you choose the background.

I have played with a few different types of backgrounds, and I like outside in the daytime best. I hook an inch or two of greens on the bottom of the mat, and the rest is mixed pale blues for sky. I like to make the grass an uneven line as this looks more organic and natural.

The background can be changed to night by darkening the greens and mixing some royal blues with navy for the night skies. Add a little gold, and you have a starry night. The sky can be hooked in swirls or in small cumulus-cloud–like areas. Either seems to have a good effect.

I also use interior scenes as the background. You can use almost any color as the floor. I sometimes will mark the area off into squares, outline the squares and hook the squares in alternate colours such as red and white, so that the floor will look like tile. The main part of the background can then be solid; sometimes I like to add diamonds or stripes to approximate wallpaper. When you start thinking of the background as wallpaper, the design possibilities become endless, like the ideas for dressing the women themselves.

These little rugs of big-boned girls have made me realize that I never really grew up. I am a child at heart, and the chance to play the kinds of games I played when I was 11 makes me happy.

Giving Back

Hooking for a cause

The Duxbury Rug Hookers, Duxbury, Massachusetts

Community involvement has always been a part of my life. I have been active in clubs and served on committees ever since I was a young girl—it is just part of who I am. As an adult, not only has rug hooking become a huge part of my life, but it also has developed into a career. Over the past 15 years I have found that the art of rug hooking, and community involvement, have blended together. When we are lucky enough to have something, such as an art or craft that we are passionate about, it is easy to use it to become involved in our communities. It helps to make them richer, healthier places in lots of ways.

A Social Activity

For some people rug hooking is a creative outlet; for others it is a way to keep their hands busy. For a craft that has rich traditions of women working alone in the kitchen beside the fire making a rug, it has blossomed into social network of people that knows no boundaries. Groups may meet online to share ideas, or sit together at the parish hall sharing wool or stories about their adventures. You need only to look online to learn of the many events and gatherings that take place around the globe that center on rug hooking. Through this hobby people have built networks of support.

How many times have you heard a new convert exclaim, "Rug hookers are the nicest people!" Well it's true, and my research for this article has once again proven to me that rug hookers are often very giving, caring people who want to spread the joy they have gotten from the craft with others. Many have a strong social conscience; others have a deep need to share with others the soothing, calming effect that hooking rugs has had in their own lives. I have met many people who told me that they worked through many personal issues thrumming their hook, and getting lost in bundles of color. In my research I have found that groups all over North America and beyond are recognizing the importance of rug hooking in their communities and using it as a tool to give back to those very localities.

The Duxbury Massachusetts Rug Hookers

Many people are using rug hooking to create, develop, and build community in healthy,

PHOTOS COURTESY OF PEG IRISH

Seven Sisters, 4' x 6', #6- and #8-cut wool on burlap. Designed and hooked by Deanne Fitzpatrick, Amherst, Nova Scotia, 1997.

- - - - - - - - - - - - - - - - - - - -

This group, like many others, meets for the joy of it, but they are also giving back. Hosting a show of hooked rugs offers an experience for people to come and see the beauty of the craft, as well as a chance to raise money for library books that they, as well as everyone else, get to enjoy. Secondly, they are giving back to the society by providing them with a place to meet.

Rug Hooking and Mental Health

Far across the Atlantic in England, Priscilla (Cilla) Cameron is busy at work creating community through rug hooking. Over the past years she has worked with mental health patients, as well as teaching rug hooking to learning-disadvantaged students. "Men and women taking part in these

therapeutic ways. Sometimes it is as simple as gathering together as a group to hook and do a little fundraising. The Duxbury Rug Hookers, a group of about 25 women, meet once a month in the Alden Kindred Barn. The Alden Society maintains this barn and the original house and property of John and Priscilla Alden. Tours are available to the public, and the barn is available for community programming. The Alden Kindred number more than a million people and are the descendants of John and Priscilla Alden. Each year the Duxbury Rug Hookers create a rug communally, which raises between $1,000 and $2,000 for the society. In addition, this year they hosted a show of their rugs in the local library, raising $400 for the purchase of craft books. Olga Rothschild, a member of the group said, "The communal rug builds a sense of togetherness which is often lacking in modern life."

- - - - - - - - - - - - - - - - - - - -

The Library Rug, 27" x 38", #3- to #8-cut wool on linen. Designed and hooked by The Duxbury Rug Hookers, Duxbury, Massachusetts, 2004.

projects may have poor social skills, little ability to write or to use rug making tools, difficulties in taking part in group projects, and very low concentration levels," says Cilla. "As an artist/teacher one must very quickly make clients feel comfortable. It can take some time for them to have confidence in you and not see you as yet another person from the system trying to analyze them." Cilla asks her clients to work in twos or threes and draw or write their favorite things. Next they collate the words and pictures into designs by making templates. With a sheet of paper the size of the rug, everyone decides where to place the templates to build the pattern, and finally, they draw around the templates and transfer the pattern to Hessian (burlap). All participants create samples to practice the technique of proddy. "Most people in England who made rugs from rags used the proddy method and are not so familiar with hooking," she says. Cilla explains that one woman was very withdrawn and never spoke to anyone. She surprised her caretaker when she started to talk about the rug making in her home as a child. "She grabbed the tool from me and proceeded to give a demonstration of how things were done in her day. It really was an amazing happening."

Cilla finds that it is best to sew the rug onto a large frame so that three or four participants can sit and work together in a relaxed atmosphere where the stories flow freely. She has found that the creation of a rug makes the participants proud, helps develop social skills, builds confidence, and brings along lots of fun and laughter. This type of work has become a very satisfying part of her career as a professional rug hooking artist and teacher.

The West Virginia Church Project

Susan Feller, of Ruckman Mill Farm, Augusta, West Virginia, has used rug hooking in several different ways to become more involved with her community. Initially she was enchanted when she saw Linda Ratcliffe demonstrating rug hooking in Romney, West Virginia, during a local open house. Together they worked with their minister at the local Methodist church to enhance the sanctuary and complement the beautiful stained glass

- -

Alden House—Plimoth Colony, *28" x 20", #6- to #8-cut wool on linen. Designed by Olga Rothschild and The Duxbury Rug Hookers. Hooked by The Duxbury Rug Hookers, Duxbury, Massachusetts, 2004.*

windows in the church. They created an 8' x 3' rug, the same size as the windows, to depict the history of the church. Susan designed the rug in panels and also dyed the wool for the rug, while Linda hooked it. In addition, another church member, Mary French Barby, hooked the paramounts—panels that hang over the lectern at the front of the church which depict the liturgical seasons. Together, these rugs, along with the stained glass, have enhanced the beauty of the church, adding yet another spiritual dimension to a sacred place.

A second community project that Susan was instrumental in developing was with a group of New Jersey Girl Scouts and Brownies. "I walked into a room of screaming girls, and left a group of rug hookers as quiet as church mice," says Susan. The Brownie leader, Lisa Minns, has just begun working with the girls to create beginner kits to sell as a fundraiser both for the Girl Scouts, and as part of an outreach program to the children of women who reside at the local women's prison.

Sharing an Understood Art

Years ago when I first started hooking rugs, I met Anne Johnson, the director of The Drew, a nursing home in New Brunswick, Canada. I was impressed with a project that she had developed for both the home and the residents.

For many years In Atlantic Canada, rug hooking was one of the few ways a woman could decorate

Hooked rug contributed by residents at Drew Nursing Home, New Brunswick, Canada.

her home. It was an inexpensive craft that even the wives of subsistence fishermen and farmers could afford. Anne decided that she would use rugs to decorate the halls of the nursing home. When residents moved in, she would offer them or their children the opportunity to hang the hooked rugs they had around their homes as art in their new home. This provided an opportunity for the residents to feel comfortable in their surroundings. She also helped establish the value of the rugs as art and to preserve them for the community. Many of these rugs would have been lost or destroyed if she had not seen their cultural importance.

Anne adds, "The value of and the interest in the mats has certainly increased in the past 25 years, and a generation of residents and staff have shared this environment. We asked ourselves if these items would continue to be important to subsequent generations or if the décor would become "dated" and disposable. In a very small way we think we have created a museum or art gallery and have consequently preserved important aspects of culture and heritage for the enjoyment of those that live and visit at the home. We want to believe these items will continue to be appropriate and valued."

The Mayo Clinic at Rochester, Minnesota

Last year a nurse from the Mayo Clinic called to order a rug-hooking pattern, and as is sometimes the case we got to talking about rug hooking and the programs that are offered by the Women's Cancer Program at the clinic. A few days later I got an email from Romayne Thompson, an occupational therapist at the clinic, with a kind note telling me how much she liked the rug that had appeared in Mary Sheppard Burton's book, *A Passion for the Creative Life*. As it turned out this rug, called *The Seven Sisters*, is one I created in the mid-1990s celebrating my six sisters; I am the youngest of seven. I had kept the rug as I could not sell it but I also could not give it to one of my sisters, or I would have five others mad at me. I enjoyed it for years and wanted to see it hanging in a public space. When Romayne told me about the fantastic programs around art and craft and healing that were taking place at the clinic, I knew that the rug would have a good home there. I liked their philosophy that arts like quilting and rug hooking could be therapeutic in both a physical and emotional way for cancer patients.

Romayne decided to take up rug hooking herself and to have a rug set up at the clinic for patients to work on. A great deal of research done over the years shows the benefits of using art as a healing tool, and it also shows that the clinic was moving forward in this direction. "Returning persons to wholeness after the shock of cancer often demands a new approach on the part of the survivor and of

The Mayflower, *24" x 30", #3- to #8-cut wool on linen. Designed by Brooks Kelly. Hooked by The Duxbury Rug Hookers, Duxbury, Massachusetts, 2003.*

the persons in the circles of their lives," says Anne. "It is our hope that by bringing old and new art forms into their lives, we can help them to discover or rediscover interests that help them in personal expression, to enhance their daily lives as they deal with the changes they have experienced," says Anne.

Hooked rug contributed by residents at Drew Nursing Home, New Brunswick, Canada.

Women at the Pithead

Springhill, Nova Scotia is perched, as its name suggests, on a hill in the center of Cumberland County, Nova Scotia, surrounded by miles of spruce woodland and blueberry fields. It is famous for being the hometown of Anne Murray, the internationally famous singer. Sadly, it is also famous for mining disasters—in 1891, 1956, and 1958—which claimed the lives of 443 people from this small community. Many people living in Springhill today remember the 1950s and the rescue operations that took place to save the miners trapped underground. Having lived in this area for over 20 years, I had it in my mind for a long time to create a mat commemorating the mining history of Springhill. Over the past five to seven years I noticed that rug hooking was becoming a big part of community life in Springhill, with two groups meeting during the day, plus an evening group. In a community of approximately 3,500 people, there were about 50 or more rug hookers. I spoke to Bea Hatfield, who has hooked many rugs, to see if she thought the women she hooked with would be interested in carrying out a commemorative project, and I offered to help in any way I could. She invited me to come to their meeting and propose the idea. I thought that to be an authentic tribute, it would make sense if the Springhillers themselves were the ones to carry out the project. They readily agreed. At our first meeting, Bea had brought along copies of the Halifax *Herald* documenting the explosions. On one of these yellowed fragile pages we saw a picture of the wives of the miners, waiting at the pithead for news of their husbands who were trapped underground. Immediately we came to a consensus that this was the subject we would use to carry out the project. The women of Springhill decided that they wanted to commemorate the strength and dignity of the women whose lives were affected by the disaster. There were many widows in Springhill who raised families on their own, having lost their husbands too early to the mine. It made sense to the rug hookers to acknowledge these members of their community with a hooked rug.

The Springhill Hookers have agreed that the rug will hang in the new Dr. Carson and Mrs. Marion

PHOTOGRAPHS COURTESY OF DEANNE FITZPATRICK

The Women Waiting at the Pithead, *5' x 6', #6- and #8-cut wool on burlap. Designed by Deanne Fitzpatrick. Hooked by the Springhill Rug Hooking Group, Springhill, Nova Scotia, 2005.*

Murray Community Center. The rug is still in progress, but will be completed this winter. They have done a beautiful job honoring the women in their community who waited, strengthened their relationship with one another, and their community will be graced with a meaningful piece of art.

Sustaining the Art of Rug Hooking

I believe that one of the ways to preserve rug hooking for future generations is to teach children how to hook. Together with their rug hooking group, Les Hookeuses au Bor-De-Lo, Line Godbout and Danielle Oulette coordinated a project that married teaching watercolor, Acadian legends, and rug hooking to 150 children in their community. Their group went into the schools and told the children an Acadian legend. The children would immediately paint their story, and then members

Rug Show at the Capital Theatre Art Gallery, Moncton, New Brunswick. Line Godbout and Danielle Oulette and their group, Les Hookeuses au Bor-de-lo, coordinated this project with 150 school children in their community to combine Acadian history with rug hooking.

of the group would transfer the 12" x 12" drawings to burlap for the children to hook. Together they created a show to hang at the Capital Theatre Art Gallery in Moncton, New Brunswick. It will also travel to Fredricton, the capital city, where it will be hosted at the New Brunswick Lieutenant Governor's residence. At the opening of the exhibit at the Capital Theatre, which was attended by over 300 people, I saw a community bubbling over with excitement. The children were excited by their work, the parents were proud, and Les Hookeuses au Bor-de-lo had a sense of accomplishment.

The group also decided to create a series of cards and prints of the mats created and they donated over $1,000 in proceeds from the cards to charity. Line Godbout said, "This has been a very positive and uplifting experience. From the beginning, there was magic underneath all aspects of this project and it seemed to take on a life of its own. The initial idea just bloomed into many different components, with everything just falling easily in place. But the energy was there because we were so motivated and proud to show not only our work, but also the children's artwork."

Becoming Involved in a Community Project

Whether you pursue rug hooking as a hobby, craft, or an art, there are tremendous opportunities to use it to build, develop, or just get involved in your community. Because it is something you love to do, it is also important to protect yourself and your art. I get many more requests for community involvement than I can possibly meet. Many people will call for a donation of a rug, or to ask for your time to teach for free. It is important to decide which groups and causes are important to you and that you want to support, because you cannot support them all.

A good community project can develop in several ways. You can work for the good of the community carrying out a project yourself, such as creating a rug to donate for a worthy cause. In this case it is important that the group you are donating to knows the value of handmade hooked rugs and can successfully use it to raise funds. A rug can also be given as a gift of art to a public institution so that many people can enjoy it. Many public organizations have no budget for artwork but really appreciate the value of it on their walls. I have found this a good option for rugs that I cannot bear to sell, but no longer have the space for in my home.

If you are involved in a project that involves many people, one of the biggest challenges may be working together. It may be necessary to have a chair or co-ordinator who is good at making sure all the voices of the group are heard and incorporated. It is like working on any project together; building consensus and moving forward can be the real task ahead of you. In the projects I have discussed, I learned that they were a success because members listened to and respected each other. Their motivation was in caring for each other as group members, caring for their community, and caring for the art of rug hooking.

Choose the projects you want to get involved in carefully, because you do not want to turn this beautiful craft into "another thing that has to be done." Use it wisely, but be sure to give it away when the time is right. It will, as the saying goes, come back to you tenfold.

Hooking Geometric Rugs

From traditional to modern

Geometric rugs are the first and easiest style of design when it comes to getting modern with our rug hooking. It is the natural go-to style when we set out to make a modern design. The interesting thing about this is that they are probably some of the oldest recorded designs of hooked rugs.

In fact, even earlier than hooked mats, Berber, Moorish, and Arabic carpets from the 16th century (Ketchum, *Hooked Rugs*, 1976) were often geometric in style, featuring cubes, rectangles, stars, and crescents with backgrounds resembling the popular hit-or-miss tradition of hooked mats. No doubt sailors and explorers returned from faraway travels with these rugs, just as we do today, and thus they influenced the design of hooked mats a century or two later.

Chevrons, *detail.*

I can only imagine how geometrics became such an enormous design style in rug hooking. It would have begun with a woman saying, "I can't draw." Then she looked at the burlap and saw that it was a grid. She started drawing lines. She took a break, made herself a cup of tea, saw the circle of the tea cup and thought, "My! I could trace this inside the lines." Ahhhh, the birth of the geometric. It is a style that evolved out of necessity much like the tradition of rug hooking itself.

Geometric designs also appeared in pattern catalogs, though they were often slightly more complex than the grids commonly designed by women in their kitchen.

Once a woman drew the geometric design of blocks or boxes, the way in which she hooked the interior of the boxes would change the design. A simple four-by-four box could be turned into a log cabin, a wave design, a zigzag pattern, or a basket weave simply by altering the direction of the hooking.

Hit and Miss Flow, *pillow. 12" x 12", 2009.*

Or perhaps she combined the geometric design with a few flowers for a geometric floral. I think this might have emerged from someone being a little bored with the straight lines and deciding to pop in a flower. I could see myself doing this.

For the standard geometric, however, one of the keys to a good design is repetition. You could take an octagon, a Greek key, or a star and repeat it again and again to create a design or pattern. Measuring was also important, making sure that the design was evenly spaced. A background was naturally created behind the design.

The square, the triangle, the octagon, the circle—whatever shape you choose has the potential to be repeated and turned into a pattern. You can change the scale of the geometric by enlarging or reducing the shape. You can combine the shapes to enhance the pattern or create a different rhythm.

Then you can enhance a geometric design with a border. The border can be solid or it, too, might have a geometric design on it. Or the border can be layered, with one design outside another.

Traditionally we think of geometrics as perfectly spaced and measured. But in the past year I have had a lot of fun using simple shapes and

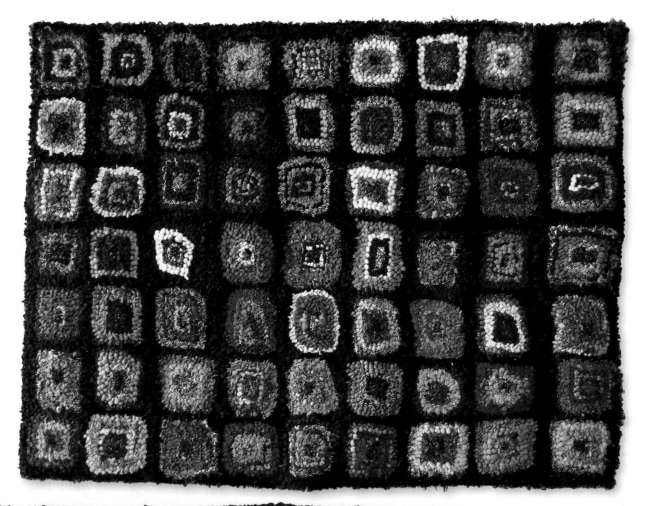

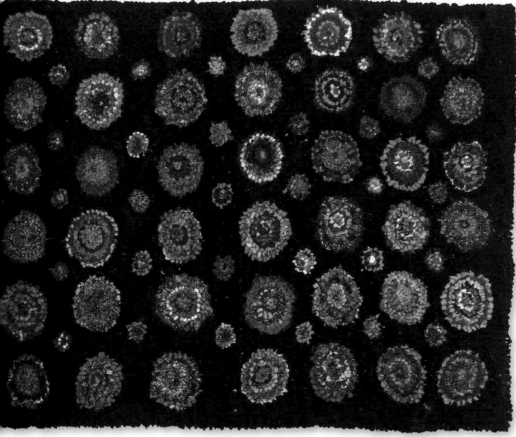

Above: **Gone Mod**, *48" x 36", wool strips on burlap. Designed and hooked by Deanne Fitzpatrick, 2005.*

Left: **Circles in Blue**, *50" x 36", 2008.*

not measuring. I refer to these as my Organic Geometrics.

The two words are kind of opposites in a way, but I have found that opposites attract and they are very good together. Instead of taking a shape and repeating it in exactly the same size evenly spaced, I have taken to drawing them in a free hand fashion so that they are not perfectly spaced or exactly the same although there is repetition and a definitive geometric quality to them. I'll look through a book such as Owen Jones' *The Grammar of Ornament*, or Ernest Haeckel's *Art Forms from the Ocean* for an inspiring shape. There are hundreds of books out there that show us shapes and forms and designs.

They are good resource books—you cannot have enough of them. I'll pore through them looking for something interesting, then change it marginally just by the fact that I drew it freehand.

I think the nature and definition of what is a geometric is changing even today. And that is as it should be. Design styles, including the geometric style, will continue to evolve. As rug hookers, we'll continue to explore the possibilities with simple shapes, arranging them, rearranging them, layering them, turning them upside down, backwards, and inside out to see where it takes us. They can still be geometrics—they'll simply just be modern geometrics.

- -

Circles in Color, *54" x 48", 2008.*

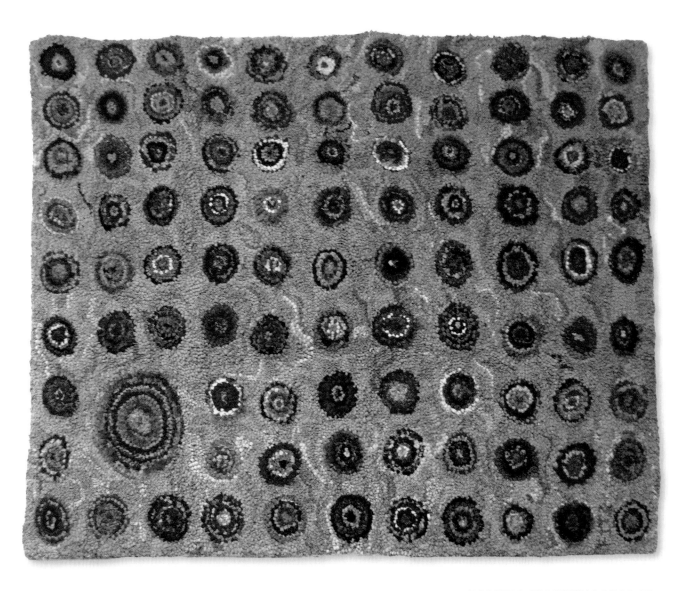

Twenty Years at the Mat

A glance backward at rug hooking's move forward

I have been hooking for 20 years. In 1990 when I learned how to hook, I was 25 years old. Rug hooking was a quiet little hobby that few people had heard of, and for many of those who knew of it, it was something their grandmothers did.

I started to hook because I wanted old-fashioned mats for the floors of my farmhouse. So I went off to a Rug Hooking Guild of Nova Scotia annual meeting in Tatamagouche with three of my sisters. There I met Doreen Wright and Marion Kennedy, who ran Rags to Rugs, the only shop in Nova Scotia to sell traditional and primitive hooked rug supplies.

Doreen and Marion were both strong-minded women, trained in a very traditional style of rug

Deanne Fitzpatrick hooked her first rug in 1990 from a Bluerose pattern. The rug is 18" x 30", #6-, #8-, and handcut wool on burlap, and it reflects the style and patterns common at the time.

hooking. They liked nice even loops, hand-dyed Dorr Wool, and a tidy style. They also had a strong affection for the traditional patterns of Nova Scotia and understood that we had a long history of mat making along our shores.

Marion, a long-time rug hooker with a gravelly voice and a gruff manner, told me, "If you want to hook, you have to finish things, so just keep at this mat until it is done." That weekend, she gave me a small mat with four scrolls in the corner, enough navy coat wool for the background, a teal green to outline the scrolls, some blue Harris Tweed sports coat to fill in the scrolls, and a basic rug hooking lesson.

Every once in a while she would come back around and look over my shoulder. I'd ask her, "Do you think I should take that out?" She'd say, "How are you ever going to finish it that way? Hook it until it's done." Looking back, I see that Marion made rug hooking easy for me. She taught me how and left me to my own devices.

Diamonds in the Sky, *24" x 34", #6-, #8-, and handcut wool, silk, velvet on burlap. Designed and hooked by Deanne Fitzpatrick, Amherst, Nova Scotia, 2009. Twenty years later, Deanne's rugs have a new, contemporary look; they are wild, colorful patterns which are a far cry from the structured first rug she hooked in 1990.*

- -

When I went back to Amherst I discovered six other rug hookers who gathered every second week to hook together. They all hooked lovely mats in a traditional style, and most were shading flowers. It was a lovely group of people and they welcomed me. I fit in very well, but it was clear that my rugs did not. I hooked like a wild banshee compared to their neat work.

When I started rug hooking, the only style around was the traditional style. It was the "way to hook," and "the *only* way to hook." But I kept asking myself, "How can there be a wrong way to carry out an art or a craft?" I knew that years ago, my grandmother had made mats in outport New-foundland using feed bags and clothing scraps. I doubt she held fast to any list of rules. I didn't either. I played a lot with materials and ideas, and rug hooking became my art. Over the next six or seven years of hooking every day, rug hooking made me an artist.

Changing Styles and Connections

From behind my frame I have seen a lot of changes over the last 20 years. When I first began hooking rugs, antiques and country style were all the rage. Today people seem interested in sparser, more contemporary designs.

Rug hooking continues to grow—in spite of the whims of fashion—for a couple of reasons. First, rug designs can be adapted and developed to reflect changing tastes and styles. And second, rug hooking is a strong cultural tradition that is about more than style; it is becoming increasingly about lifestyle. As the world speeds up, rug hookers choose their craft in an effort to slow down. It is a purposeful response to a demanding world. We sit at the mat to relax and to reflect. It is our own private retreat that we can carry with us in a big canvas bag.

One piece of modern life that we are retreating from, computerization, ironically is speeding up the pace of rug hooking's growth. The advent of the Internet has meant that people can learn how to hook rugs in five minutes by watching a video on YouTube. I have posted three videos myself in the last several months. The first has had nearly 9000 viewers. Twenty years ago, creating a video was a huge expensive project; now all it takes is a teenager and a cheap digital camera.

The Internet means that we learn tips and ideas from each other at an accelerated pace. We can access a large community with many different ideas and thoughts about rug hooking. It is easy to learn that there are many right ways to hook. It also means that rules and standards about rug hooking are harder to abide by, and even more difficult to enforce. The Internet broadens our sense of community, and though it is only a virtual community, it does give us a chance to find a community that is supportive of the types of rugs we like to make. In my experience, guilds and rug hooking groups have responded positively and are open and enthusiastic about new ideas in rug hooking, including those we find on the Internet. What was once considered breaking the rules is now seen as creativity.

Shoes and Skirts, *36" x 16", #6-, #8-, and handcut wool on burlap. Designed and hooked by Deanne Fitzpatrick, Amherst, Nova Scotia, 2009.*

Contemporary Rug Hooking

That is one of the biggest changes I have seen in the twenty years I have been hooking: people no longer believe that they need follow a lot of rules. The online community and the grassroots movement of being taught by your neighbor encourage people to design, and to dye their own wool—two more positive changes in the growth of rug hooking.

When Helen Serrao, past president of the Rug Hooking Guild of Nova Scotia, started hooking, a single shop sold supplies in Atlantic Canada. Now nearly a dozen small studios teach, promote, and sell supplies. "The greatest change is people doing their own thing," she said. "I think is absolutely amazing, and much more artistic." She has seen color trends move from pastels and subtle shading to much bolder statements. "More young people are getting involved because the guild teachers are doing more interesting stuff—not just what my grandmother did. Today rug hooking is more upbeat, more today." A number of exciting teachers are turning people on to the craft, making rug hooking much more than a leftover from days past.

September's Glory, 4' x 2¹/₂', #3- and 4-cut wool on Scottish burlap. Designed and hooked by Brenda Clarke, Amherst, Nova Scotia, 1998. Hooked in a class by Jeanne Field, this fine-shaded rug has a whipped, corded edge and uses 6- and 7-value swatches and dip dyes.

We love the history and tradition, and we love the new contemporary look.

The schools hosted by the Rug Hooking Guild of Nova Scotia have been extremely important in building the momentum behind rug hooking's growth. The guild has over 1,000 members, many of whom live outside the immediate area. People become members to attend the school and receive the newsletter. Then they carry rug hooking back to their own communities.

Rugs as Art

The strong resurgence of rug hooking has created an interest in rugs as art. Rugs have jumped off the floor and landed on the walls of galleries, public institutions, and homes. Many rug hookers show

Fish School, 18" x 42", #5- and 6-cut wool and yarn on linen. Designed by Deanne Fitzpatrick and hooked by Brenda Clarke, Amherst, Nova Scotia, 2009. This wide cut primitive rug is an example of coloring with yarn. About half of the rug is hooked with wool strips, while the border and various parts of each fish are hooked in yarn, some of which was hand spun and hand dyed. Water droplets on the fish were hooked with glitter yarn. Fish School reflects contemporary color and style in hooked rugs.

their work in provincial, state, and national galleries. As a result, the discussion about whether hooked rugs can be considered art has been rendered a moot point: they are art.

About 12 years ago, I spoke at an exhibit of hooked rugs at The Canadian Museum of Civilization. One of the rugs in the exhibit was hooked by the famous Canadian painter, Emily Carr; others were hooked by an old man in his shed in rural Quebec. The cross-section of work was phenomenal. After my speech, I met Mary Sheppard Burton, the esteemed American rug hooking artist and author of *A Passion for the Creative Life, Textiles to Lift the Spirit.* Having spent her lifetime creating and hooking rugs, she saw an even deeper importance in this exhibit. She talked about the great potential for growth in rug hooking and she said, "Honey, you got a tiger by the tail."

Since then, Mary has swung the tail of the tiger herself. She created a beautiful coffee table book about rug hooking. Her collection of 12 hooked rugs depicting stories passed down through her family was acquired by the American Folk Life Centre in 2006. Her hooked sculpture, *Noah's Ark,* is spectacular. "I am so lucky to be able to do this, to hook rugs every day," she said. Like many of her contemporaries—Doris Eaton, Joan Moshimer, and other strong women who were part of the early rug hooking resurgence in the 1970s—Mary saw that rug hooking was a rich and vibrant craft that had an exciting future. Their efforts paved the way to the joyous, raucous, exciting craft that rug hookers enjoy today.

Hooking Skies

Swirls and paisleys add drama

Nothing makes you realize how very small you are like looking up to the sky. No matter when you look—on a stormy day, a starry night, or a mauve summer evening—you see that the sky is not still. It is ever-changing and moody.

Hooking the sky and capturing those moods takes a lot of practice. It also takes a lot of attention. You have to notice what the skies look like, how they change depending on the weather, and how the time of day alters their appearance.

Take Time for Observation

Before you hook a sky, go outside and look up. You'll see many different types of clouds: Cumulus clouds are big, heaping, fluffy clouds. Stratus clouds are thinly layered clouds. Cirrus clouds are like big curls of hair. Nimbus clouds are heavier-looking rain clouds. What kind of clouds best suit the day you want to depict? What time of day are you trying to capture? These are simple but important considerations.

Notice where the light is coming from and where it hits. Not being aware of this natural phenomenon

If You Want to Hook the Sky . . .

- Think about the weather before you start the sky. The weather affects the color of the sky.
- Avoid hooking straight across. The sky is full of movement, so use movement in your hooking to get that feeling. Draw swirling lines on your rug to guide you.
- Pick blues, but don't underestimate the power of other colors to create mood, such as pale greens, mauves, pale yellows, and grays.
- Natural sheep's wool fleece is perfect for clouds, but do not hook it in perfect ovals; try hooking it in odd, irregular shapes.
- Remember to change the direction of your hooking. Skies call for motion in your hooking. This technique is hard to get used to, but the result is great skies.
- Be liberal with creams and whites. Some days the sky has more cloud cover than blue. ■

So Small under a Big Sky, *48" x 58", #6-, 8-, and hand-cut wool cloth and yarn on burlap. Designed and hooked by Deanne Fitzpatrick, Amherst, Nova Scotia, Canada, 2009.*

The sky is a playground, and I filled it with paisleys. Paisleys are fun to hook if you do not hold yourself to a pattern. Hook each one as its own little work of art.

is a common mistake in pictorial rugs. For example, the landscape in a rug may be hooked in bright and sunny colors, but the sky is gray. This inconsistency might confuse the viewer: where is the light coming from? The type of sky has to match the type of light that shows on the ground.

The next time you see a beautiful sunset, notice the interaction among the colors in the sky. Sometimes rug hookers hook sunsets in lines straight across their backing, but all the viewer ends up seeing is the direction of the hooking rather than the sky itself. When you hook in straight lines, it is hard to blend the shades of the wool together.

Facing: **Winter Sky**, *20" x 36", #6-, 8-, and hand-cut wool cloth and yarn on burlap. Designed and hooked by Deanne Fitzpatrick, Amherst, Nova Scotia, Canada, 2005.*

The drama in this rug is all in the sky. You can really use the sky as an area to play with and fill with intensity. I drew these big swirls, hooked them first, and then filled in the background. It suggests a stormy sky.

Instead, one color ends abruptly and another begins. Rather than a nice, blended sunset, the result is a choppy sky.

Sky Tip

Skies are some of the more interesting areas of the mat to hook, but they take practice. Why not create a set of samplers for yourself? Take four small pictorials—it can even be the same pattern—and hook each one with a different style of sky. Try a rug that is 10" by 14", perhaps with a single small house in the corner, and hook the rest in sky. We learn by doing, and with each sky we hook, we are more prepared for the next one.

Stormy Sky

- A stormy sky is not just a gray sky. It is made up of shades of grays and blues and creams.
- A stormy sky has lots of motion and movement. It is an unsettled sky that has a lot of drama.
- Use dark colors to emphasize the heaviness of the impending storm. Deep shades of gray, gray-blue, and gray-green really emphasize that heavy feeling.
- Clouds in the stormy sky could be pale yellow or lightest gray or cream to accentuate that unsettled feeling.

Night Sky

- Use a navy wool as the base of the night sky and add two or three other similar, but slightly brighter, shades of navy with it. Throw in some black, dark green, or purple for highlights.
- Hook tiny circles of yellow or white, two or three loops each, for stars.
- Throw in some multicolored mohair yarns with red, blue, pink, etc.
- Hook the sky from the ground toward the top of the sky in big jagged thick lines, always starting and finishing in different places. ■

Gathering the right selection of yarns is important. Look for variegated blues in a variety of textures.

You can see many shades very close together, highlighted with fleece for clouds, and a darker mauve for depth.

I use many shades of sky blue for a sky. Often they are so close together that the variation is only slight. I like how they hook up together.

Vines in the Field, *60" x 52", #6-, 8-, and hand-cut wool cloth and yarn on burlap. Designed and hooked by Deanne Fitzpatrick, Amherst, Nova Scotia, Canada, 2004.*

There is an upward motion of hooking in this sky. I hooked in small patches toward the outside edge of the rug, as if the sky was going off the rug. To me, this implies an expansiveness to the sky that is beyond what is shown.

A Realistic Approach to Hooking Skies

I take many different approaches to hooking skies, depending on the feeling I want to convey. Sometimes I want to convey the sky exactly the way I see it. When I hook it in a realistic way, I usually take fleece (natural sheep's wool) and hook in the clouds first. I hook the clouds in all directions: up, down, and across. You can hook three loops over, turn down two loops, then go back four loops, then back two. Any pattern can work. I then add the same color again, going back and forth, up and down, and filling in. Think of it like baking biscuits: you can change the ingredients a bit and you still get nice fluffy biscuits.

When I don't want really fluffy clouds, I use a white wool cloth or a sweater. Strips cut from wool sweaters make great clouds because they curl as you hook them. They are full without being overpowering, and they add interest because the

Moon over County Road, *36" x 22", #6-, 8-, and hand-cut wool cloth and yarn on burlap. Designed and hooked by Deanne Fitzpatrick, Amherst, Nova Scotia, Canada, 2009.*

I love thin cirrus clouds and added bits of mauve against a background blue-gray sky. The moon works well in a bit of mixed creams. I find a loosely woven sweater hooks up well for the moon.

viewer cannot immediately identify what material the rug hooker used. I follow the same method of hooking as I did with the fleece, but I change materials and colors a bit. A cloud becomes more interesting because the various shades and textures appear as a play on light. Try colors like pale yellows, creamy mauves, pale grays, and a variety

of whites and creams. Always remember: your color choices depict mood, time of day, and light.

Once the clouds are hooked, I add the colors of the sky. For a bright sunny day, I might choose four or five shades of pale blue. Sometimes I'll throw in a bright mauve. I hook the sky the same way I hook the clouds, but in larger areas. I often

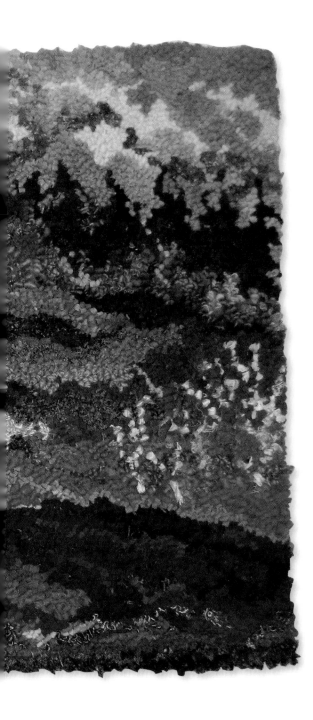

Hooking
the Evening Sky

- Color is the key to communicating the time of day. For evening sky, blue with a pink cast or mauve will take you there. Gather some midblues and a complementary mauve and hook them together. I use three swatches of blues to one swatch of mauve.
- Think of evening skies as long stretches of color, not hooked across in straight lines, but in longer, narrow swaths. ■

and textures in big fluffy areas, similar to cumulus clouds. I never leave straight hard edges. I round them off instead.

Because I hook with a loose, big stitch, using #6- and #8-cut wool, I can blend the colors together as I hook. When I am introducing a new color up against another, I hook tightly because I want one color to blend into the other. It is the old idea of fingering used among flower shaders, except instead of fingers of wool loops, these are wobbly lines of wool loops.

I choose colors that are very close together. They can be several shades of any color, depending on the type of sky I want to create. The beauty of having the colors close together is that the mixing becomes very easy and the shading is incredibly subtle. You can only really see the beauty of the shading when the rug is done and you step away from it and see it as a whole. Trust me on this: it works with grays, mauves, deep blues, and a variety of other colors. I have hooked this type of sky over 100 times. Probably even more than that, because I love these strong skies.

A Lighter Approach

Other times, in other rugs, the sky is an area that should be whimsical. Start to think of the sky not as part of the landscape, but as a place to be

think of the sky as a big series of clouds all mashed together, but some are blue. This approach is relaxing because you are really hooking one step—or one cloud—at a time.

The "big blue sky" is one of my favorite skies to hook. For that sky I choose three to ten colors of pale blue that are fairly close together. (Almost any number of shades is fine, if you keep the colors close together.) Some of the shades can be different textures. For example, a bouclé wool cloth, yarn, and fleece work well together. Hook these colors

Peaks to the Sky, *58" x 64", #6-, 8-, and hand-cut wool cloth and yarn on burlap. Designed and hooked by Deanne Fitzpatrick, Amherst, Nova Scotia, Canada, 2005.*

Circles and paisleys meet in this sky. You will see that each circle or paisley is unique and contains many different colors—some of the colors you would not expect to find, like lime green. Surprise and added interest make this sky.

- -

creative and expressive. This approach has led me to a lot of delightful designs. I hook the sky as if it were a playground. I have filled huge skies with paisleys, diamonds, or circles—just for the pleasure of it.

A whimsical sky gives the rug a more contemporary feel. The viewer is attracted to the sky by the patterns. The pattern lures his eye upward.

Facing: **The Words Between Us**, *16" x 24", #6-, 8-, and hand-cut wool cloth and yarn on burlap. Designed and hooked by Deanne Fitzpatrick, Amherst, Nova Scotia, Canada, 2008.*

Here the sky is used as an expressive space. The swirls come right out of the mouths as if the light in the sky is the words between them. Look at the navy and see how many colors actually highlight it. Do not limit yourself to a small palette when hooking night skies.

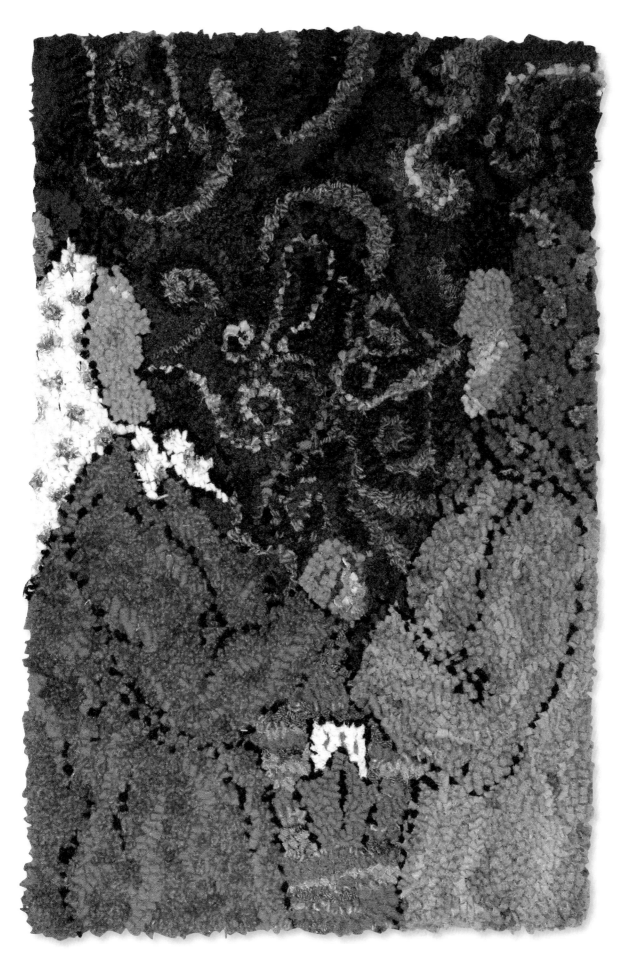

Out on the Barrens, *44" x 54", #6-, 8-, and hand-cut wool cloth and yarn on burlap. Designed and hooked by Deanne Fitzpatrick, Amherst, Nova Scotia, Canada, 2009.*

The light gray backgrounds on these paisleys soften them and make them less playful and more ponderous. Keep the background behind paisleys fairly solid. Some variegation is fine, but you do not want it to compete with the paisleys. This particular paisley sky suggests an impending storm.

For me, pattern in the sky is a play on the traditional pictorial, making rugs more fun. It takes something that is so strong in rug hooking—the use of repetitive design—and pushes the edges of the mat a little further along. I discovered this one day when faced with a big sky to hook. I had no idea if it would work, but I thought it was worth a try. It worked so well that I have continued to play with the idea for the last two years.

Paisleys
in the Sky

- First draw the shape of the paisley, circles, diamonds, or other unique shapes on the area you want to be the sky.
- Truncate some of the shapes. Allow half of a circle to come out to the edge of your rug. This design technique adds interest.
- Mix shapes. I like to mix circles and paisleys together. Use shapes that complement each other. But be careful: too many different shapes get too busy and distract from the mat.
- Shapes add a magical quality to the sky. They take the rug from impressionism or realism to playfulness. ▪

As you start your next sky, be fearless. Remember, if it doesn't work well, you can always start again. Start thinking of your rug as a series of spaces that need to be filled, and you never know where your imagination might take you.

Are You a Wild Posy or a Traditional Rose?

Hooking flowers with nature in mind

Two of my favorite flowers to hook are what I call the traditional rose and the wild posy. My love of traditional roses comes from the fact that it reminds me of my mother. It is one of the images my mother liked to hook. It is a common medallion in the center of so many Atlantic Canadian mats hooked in the early 1900s, and it reminds me of everything rug hooking is about.

The wild posy, on the other hand, reminds me of myself. It is going in all directions, loves vivid color, and might pop up anywhere. It is not traditional in any sense of the word, yet it is still a floral motif, so it still belongs.

-- -- -- -- -- -- -- -- -- -- -- -- -- -- --

Traditional Floral, *30" x 18", 2005.*

Rose Chairpad,
13" diameter, 2005.

Whether I am hooking flowers, hit and miss, abstracts, or a traditional pattern rugs are imbued with meaning. For years I had a little book that showed what every flower was a symbol of. There can be as much meaning in a floral rug as there is in a story rug. On Wikipedia or other online sites, you can find lists of plants and their meanings. It is an interesting place to begin when you are hooking floral rugs. A poppy, for example, is a symbol of pleasure. This can easily be seen in the sensuous nature of its petals, the depth of its color. Columbine, on the other hand, represents faithlessness and deceived lovers. Imagine such an intricately structured beauty representing such a thing.

Floral rugs come in all kinds of designs. You can hook them close-up and detailed or far away. You can choose a field of flowers or a vase on a table. They can be domestic or natural. I have experimented with many floral designs over the years and I cannot say I have a favorite. I weave my way in and out of the various designs depending on my mood and the time of year.

When you design a floral rug, you must decide whether you are doing a macro design, which will might be a close-up of a particular flower or flowers, a domestic setting of flowers in the home, a field of wild flowers, a garden, or various other possibilities. Florals are not just one type of rug, and each type of floral requires different treatment.

Different treatments mean that you need different line drawings and different wools and textures. You will want to have some interesting yarns, some

Traditional Rose, *choose three colors very close to each other and an outline color that contrasts. You can outline the whole flower, then use one color in each petal for simplicity. I like to mix two colors in one petal, and keep changing the combinations as I hook around the flower.*

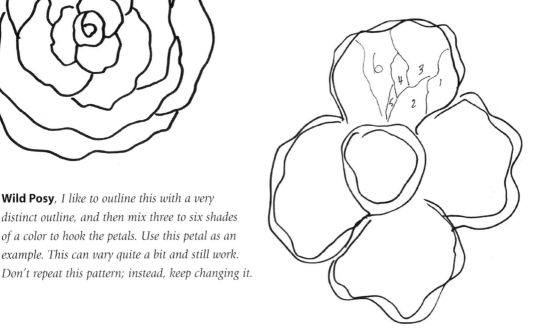

Wild Posy, *I like to outline this with a very distinct outline, and then mix three to six shades of a color to hook the petals. Use this petal as an example. This can vary quite a bit and still work. Don't repeat this pattern; instead, keep changing it.*

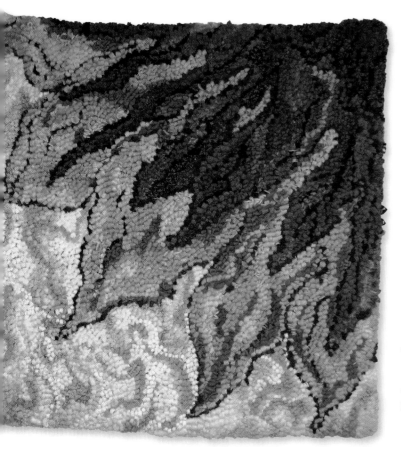

silk, some fleece, and some wool cloth on hand for hooking florals if you want to create depth and texture in your rugs. Remember color always reflects feeling and mood, so the colors you choose will determine the mood of the piece. For example, a black rose will feel much different than a yellow rose. However, it is not just the color of the flowers themselves; it is also the colors that you use in the background or the surrounding landscape that will determine the feeling the rug conveys.

The Sunflower

- I like to make the petals quite raggedy with lots of movement.
- I look for gold, but also shades of yellow for the petals because the yellow shows light.

Sunflower, *20" x 20", 2008.*

- For the centers, I look for a brown tweed or a variegated brown yarn.
- Because the petals are long, I hook them in longer curved lines going from the center to the tip of the petals rather than across. The lines should be organically shaped.

Big Close-Ups of Flowers

- Focus on the center—this will draw the eye.
- Sometimes the center of the flower will have several colors, or a decorative elements of dots that lets me add a little texture or an interesting yarn.
- I like to outline the center in a couple of contrasting colors.
- Use several shades of one color in each petal to add dimension and interest so the flower will not appear flat.

Big Blooms, *20" x 22", 2014.*

Floral Arrangements

- If you are hooking flowers in a vase, consider how you plan to make the flowers contrast with the vase and the background, and with the table or ground upon which it is laid.
- This takes considerably more color planning than just mixing the flowers with some green. There may be many elements competing with each other: a patterned cloth or wallpaper, and a vase that may or not be patterned.
- Make sure you make the flowers distinguishable. This is usually done by outlining them in a distinctive color.

Left: **Basket of Posies**, *12" x 10", 2013.*
Below: **Painter's Garden #1**, *24" x 24", 2015.*

Summer Blooms Pillow, *15" x 15", 2011.*

Smaller Flowers

- Fleece is perfect to give you the effect of flowers, as fleece raises itself higher than cloth.
- You can hook two or three loops of a color in an irregular shape, then hook a tiny bit of bright green beside it to get the effect of a flower. When you hook the background in, those colors will magically appear as flowers.
- I sometimes like to hook one loop of a bright color then add a circle of color around it to show a flower with a center.
- Change the shape of your hooking: make some long cylinder shapes, some teeny tiny round

Poppies Before the Field, *12" x 12", 2013.*

dots, and some larger dots. This will give the effect of many different types of flowers and appear as a garden.

Fields of Flowers

- Hook amoeba-like areas in one, two, or three colors that are very similar to each other to create the effect of a field of flowers or a garden.
- Make sure the areas are very irregular for a natural look.
- In the foreground of the field, be sure to add some more realistic-looking flowers, as this will create a sense of depth and perspective.

Hooking flowers, like all types of rug hooking, takes practice. The more you hook them, the better the flow of ideas and the more creative and inventive you will become. When I hook fields of flowers, I think less about the shape of the flowers and more about how the colors and textures change in a large expanse of land. When I hook a close-up of a flower, I think of the intricate centers of flowers I have seen when I took the time to peer close up in a garden.

Nature itself is the best learning ground if you want to get good at hooking and designing flowers. Spend an hour or two driving the countryside if you plan to hook a field. If you want to hook a particular flower, visit a garden and really look at the petals and the centers of particular flowers.

If you are like me, you may want to hook mythical flowers like the wild posy. To do this I would suggest looking at traditional flower shapes and abstracting them a little. I love looking at the work of fabric and stationery designers to see how they change floral images and refine them down to the simplest of forms. They inspire me to do the same. Take a traditional flower and look at it differently. How can you simplify the lines and create a beauty that is all your own?

This is the challenge of designing and hooking flowers. Start your research by spending a bit of time in a garden. Isn't that one of the nicest ways to research? Get your palette ready, pull out your sketch book, or be dangerous and start sketching right on the linen. I always tell people that you can always turn it over and start again.

- -

Spring Blooms Pillow, *8" x 22", 2014.*

Twenty Tips Learned in Over Twenty Years

I have been in the rug hooking business for 23 years and a rug hooker for 25 years. Like many people, after a couple of years of rug hooking I was inspired to create a little home-based business. I had an armoire full of supplies that I sold out of my front room and, slowly, each year I reinvested what I earned. That business grew into a downtown studio that employs nine people and is open year round.

In my 23 years in business I have seen many people start a little side business in rug hooking. They would teach, dye wool, sell supplies, design and sell patterns, sell their rugs, etc. Some have stayed the course over the long haul while other tried it for a few years and decided it was not worth the bother or were distracted by other interests. Running a business, even a tiny one, is both a rewarding and a challenging experience. If you are thinking about a rug hooking business or already have one here, are some thoughts I would like to share with you. These are some of the most important things I have learned from being in business.

1 **Know your values and stick to them.** A small business is a personal thing and it is important that the values of your business reflect you and your values. Do only what you feel is right and honest in your heart. Do what you feel is right for you, not just for your business. You will live with your business decisions in a very personal way, so make sure they sit right with you.

2 **Brand your products in a consistent way that fits well with you and your values.** My rugs have a certain look and that look has become my brand, so it is important to spread that look across my products, my online presence, my advertising, my marketing, and my studio. I make sure my web address is written on every piece of paper that goes out of the studio. Because I am an artist and my work is recognizable, I have had some flexibility in this, yet I have been consistent in getting *www.hookingrugs.com* on everything we do. I have also made sure that the values of my brand mesh well with my values. I am not the brand, but it reflects upon me, and I need to feel comfortable with it.

3 **Find great suppliers you can rely on.** Your suppliers are proprietary information and business owners hold that information close to their chest. I cannot tell you how many times random people who I do not know have called me and asked where I get my supplies. A good supplier is hard to find. Often it takes years of research to find where to buy a good product wholesale. Other times you just come across it by accident. Either way, once you have a good supplier for a product you are not going to divulge it. If you are looking for suppliers, do your research yourself: in trade magazines, online, etc. Do not expect your competition to offer you advice on this. Also, respect

your suppliers: you need them as much as they need you, because you depend on their product to earn your money.

4 *Nurture your passion.* Many people get in business because they are passionate about their art or craft. Once they begin a business they discover that it involves more than just their passion. There are many parts of running a business based on your passion that can distract you from that passion. Make sure you take the time to keep designing, creating, and making, because this will be the backbone of your business. Without your passion for it, you will lose your drive. Take time out to create and to feed your creative soul. You will need inspiration—make sure you get it.

5 *Make space for yourself.* Particularly if you have a home-based business you will need office and studio space. It can be a corner of the dining room, but make sure you have a dedicated spot where you can work freely whenever you have time. That way, you will not have time to pull everything out and put it away again and again.

6 *Let home be home.* Be careful that your home-based business does not take over your home. If it starts to, then it is time to reassess your needs. I left my business in my home a few years too long. I had rolls of wool under every bed and the spare room was full of my gear. It got so that my business was taking over the barn and half the house. People were coming and going from my back door and though I did not notice it at the time, our privacy was impinged upon. Once I moved my business into town, a softness of being fell over the house, and home became home and work became work.

7 *Change is scary but necessary for growth.* A lot of changes I made, including moving from a home-based business to town, were scary. I could not predict how things would work out, but I learned to have faith. The more times I made changes, the easier they got. Business requires change. Your customers will change. They will want new and different products, ideas, and inspiration. Your suppliers will come and go. You will change. Your tastes will evolve and your interests will diversify. Learn to embrace change because your business will require it.

8 *Be inventive.* Do not copy others. Not only do you need to get used to change, but you will find that you will need to change your products. This will only come naturally if you follow Rule #2 and nurture your creative passion. As long as you are making and creating, new ideas for new products will emerge. If you do not stay engaged in making and creating yourself, you'll be looking to others to inspire your creativity, and you'll be following instead of leading. Write down all the ideas that come to you while creating—and play

----

Yarn, wool, and more yarn

The studio entrance is inviting—and intriguing.

with them. Product development is an important part of growing a creative business. People will tire of the same old products. They are always looking for new ideas.

9 ***Be original.*** To be original you need to mine your own self for ideas as well as create experiences for yourself. Think about who you are and do some personal reflection on what you want to express. The only way you will ever be truly original is if you are expressing yourself, and expressing yourself takes some personal work: you need to know who you are and what you have to give. It also takes a great deal of playing, inventing, and making.

10 ***You need social media.*** You may not need every form of it, but find one or two that works for you. Facebook, Twitter, Pinterest, Instagram, and YouTube are all good ways of communicating with people. You do not have to be on every platform in a strong way, but I think it is good to sign up for each of them and understand

them and have an account, just in case. I have focused on YouTube and Facebook for my social media because that is where my customers hang out. However, I do have accounts on the other platforms that I think are important, and in some cases, I have them connected to each other so that I can post on one platform and send to the others.

11 ***Keep an email list of all your customers and ask their permission to contact them.*** Keeping contact with my customers through email has been really useful to me. I never add anyone to the list without their permission and I make it easy for them to unsubscribe from my emails by using email programs such as Constant Contact or MailChimp. When you go to shows, have a sign-up form. Whenever you sell something, encourage people to sign up for the newsletter or email list. Keep in touch with your customers. Once they have given you permission to contact them, they want to hear from you.

12 *Care about your customer.* Create a culture of hospitality and welcome them to your business. I respect my customers, knowing that they allow me to do what I love. That makes them really important to me. I try to put myself in their shoes and empathize with them. Occasionally you will have a problem with a customer. Try to resolve it so that they are satisfied. You will feel better and so will they. Your customers keep your business going. Some will become friends, some will return again and again. You need them for your business to work.

13 *Stay on top of the checkbook.* Always know how much money you have in the account and how much you can afford to spend. Watch your spending on a daily or at least biweekly basis so that you know how much inventory you can afford to order, or how much you can spend on staffing, etc. Try not to go into overdraft—but have one just in case you need it.

14 *Reinvest in your business.* Every year, even when I was making very little, I put money back into the business so that it would be better for myself, the people who worked there, and my customers. I grew my inventory, enhanced my decor, enlarged my space, bought equipment, or whatever we needed. The old adage, "You have to spend money to make money," is true for me.

15 *Hire help.* I found that by hiring people to do the things I was not good at or no longer liked doing, I freed up time to learn or be creative. I always hire people for short-term projects so that we can get to know each other and see

----

Come on in—think, relax, create!

if we work together well. If it is a good fit and they like the work, we can make it more permanent. I want to work with people who share similar values and ideas about customer service, people who will have a positive impact on the business. Everyone has different gifts, and it important that you get the right fit for both you and them. I have a lot of respect for my employees: they are a big part of my community and I feel as if we are working together. I listen to them and often take their advice.

16 *Get sound financial advice.* Make sure you keep all your receipts, keep good records, and have crackerjack financial support to keep your books in order. If you are not good at this, hire it out—because not being good at it can get you into a lot of trouble with cash flow and taxes. Make sure you follow the rules of your state or business for setting up and filing all provincial/state sales and income taxes and that you pay these remittances first, even before you pay yourself.

17 *Pay yourself.* It is important that you get some financial rewards from your business and you should get in the habit of writing yourself a check. I have seen people who overpaid themselves and people who reinvested everything back into their business. Neither is good. After a few years in business you should be paying yourself something. If you do not, you may find yourself frustrated and disillusioned. There are times I wrote myself a check even when I could not afford it and saved it to cash it when I had money in the account.

18 *Educate yourself.* Be a lifelong learner. Teach yourself new technology. Listen to podcasts about marketing, sales, and other business topics. Take online courses, go to classes and workshops, read books on the topic. Make sure you do not fall behind when it comes to your area of interest or business. Money spent on learning is well spent. My friends say that if you get one idea from a book you paid $25 for then your money was well spent because a good idea is worth way more than $25. Never stop learning.

19 *Price right and review it.* There is no magic formula for pricing your hooked rugs or any handmade product. Look at competitor's pricing and know the going rates and consider what the market will bear. Look at your own product to see its uniqueness and special qualities before you decide your pricing. Factor in the cost of materials and your time, then add something for your talent and uniqueness. With my hooked rugs I always ask myself: "What is it worth to me to sell it?" That simple question is where you need to be really honest with yourself. Some people would rather sell at lower prices and sell many; others would rather sell at higher prices and sell fewer. Either strategy is fine. I never wanted to overprice my rugs because I wanted many people to be able to afford them.

20 *Be honest and tell the truth.* Genuineness is the real thing and everyone is looking for the real thing. In my studio we are just ourselves—there is no putting on the dog, other than to be a bit hospitable. When you tell the truth, there is no second guessing. When you are just being yourself, it makes life and business so much easier. I have discovered that people love honesty and kindness and that they should be used together to make business better for everyone.

You live and breathe your business because of the passion you have for it. That passion is what makes the difference between you and your competition.

If you have been thinking about beginning a rug hooking business and you feel passionate about it, I encourage you to try it. I have learned so much, met so many fine people, and had the opportunity to share my ideas and experiences with many people. This in itself has made me happy and enriched my life. Twenty-three years later, I still wake up each day excited about the possibilities of teaching and learning, and I wonder who will walk in the door today and begin to change their life by learning how to hook rugs. You can't beat that.

Simply Rug Hooking

Loop by loop, we make something lovely

From the early days of my rug hooking I have been romanced by its simplicity. I started hooking rugs as a purist. I gathered burlap bags used for coffee and lentils at the Lebanese food store in Halifax. I used only recycled wool. I had one single hook. I sewed my black binding around the edges with a Singer treadle sewing machine. Everything I did was the way my grandmother would have done it. This lasted for about five years. I started out like this because at the time I was learning and, truthfully, I had very little extra cash as we were settling into our first (and only) home. Most of our money went for the basics such as new windows.

It was not just about money though; it was about the challenge of finding and gathering fabrics and maintaining the family tradition. My mother told me stories of the mats she made as a child. My father described the rugs his mother made in the

Chevrons, 3' x 5', wool strips on linen. Designed and hooked by Deanne Fitzpatrick, 2010.

kitchen of their home in Paradise, Placentia Bay, Newfoundland.

I left my Newfoundland home unwillingly as a teenager when my parents relocated to Nova Scotia, so connecting with the stories of my family's past became really important. I loved that I was doing the same craft as both my grandmothers, that my own mother had hooked as a child. It connected me to my Newfoundland roots and my family history. It was as simple as that in the beginning, and in many ways it remains that simple, 25 years later.

Simplicity is a much overused word today. It is seen as a cure for all the ills of the world and the pain of technology. But in truth, simplicity is a rather complicated thing. Isn't that an oxymoron? If simplicity were easy, we would not be talking about it so much. If simplicity were easy, we would not have to work so hard to attain it.

There is an exception to that, however, in rug hooking. In its purest form, rug hooking is a simple activity of pulling strips of wool, loop by loop, through burlap. It is not something we have to work at simplifying. Rather it is something we have to try not to complicate. Over the years, I have taught over a thousand people how to hook rugs here at the frame in my studio, and many more online, and through my videos and books. Often when I show them how to hook a rug the reaction is, "Is that it?" They cannot believe the simplicity of the technique. I remember myself as a 24-year-old learning from Marion Kennedy, who taught me the exact same thing. "I must have to knot or tie it," I said. She responded, "You just have to hook the rug and finish it."

- -

Hit and Miss, *15' x 3', wool strips on linen. Designed and hooked by Deanne Fitzpatrick, 2011.*

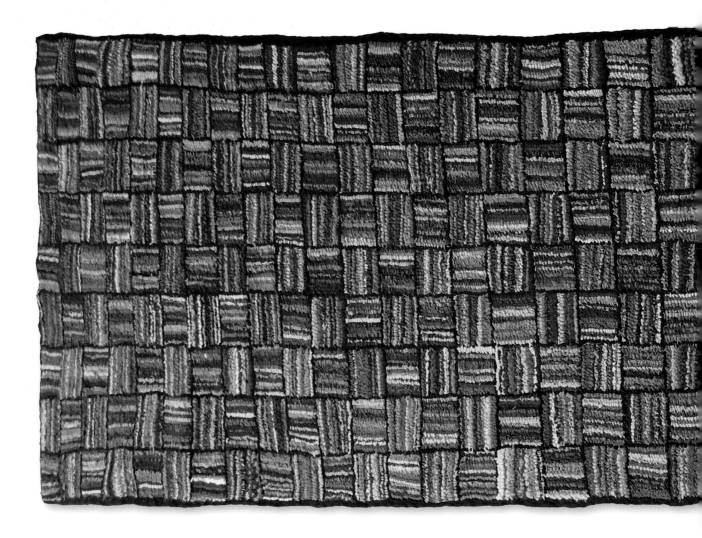

I still try to teach this way. I encourage beginners to stick with a simple design and "just finish" their first piece. I tell them, "There is only one stitch." Hearing this relieves them, lowering their stress and making them believe, "I can do this."

The act of hooking a rug has not changed since the first mat was made. It remains a simple craft that requires no electricity, no special tools—just a piece of linen or burlap, some wool, a frame, and a hook. You can do it even when the power is out.

Over the years, I have watched people complicate rug hooking. I have also watched myself complicate rug hooking. It can become as big and as complicated as we want it to, but that is a choice. Whatever rules we apply to it are of our own making. Whatever creativity we imbue it with is our own choice. When it comes right down to it, the act of making a rug is simplicity itself.

The beauty of this is that making rugs can help us maintain simplicity in our lives. Rug hooking can help us center ourselves, in the same way other people use yoga, walking, or meditation. I have practiced all three of those and I find that rug hooking is as valuable to me as any of them in terms of feeling grounded. Over the years, I have often turned to hooking when I was unsettled,

edgy, sad, lonely, bored, or any number of other unpleasant feelings. It nourishes me and helps me regain balance and wellbeing.

It makes perfect sense: To hook rugs, you usually sit quietly with yourself, you are still, you let your thoughts come and go peacefully as you pull up the loops. Myself, I always found that with meditation I had to really work at letting the thoughts come and go, while it happens naturally while rug hooking. The truth is, the simple act of sitting and hooking slows us down, gives us time to gather our thoughts, and gets us closer to simplicity. Rug hooking is simplicity itself.

In writing my new book, *Simply Modern*, published last fall by Nimbus Publishing, I spent two years exploring very simple patterns for hooked rugs, and I was amazed at what a challenge it can be to simplify color plans and designs. The act of rug hooking itself may be simple, but it is an active choice to keep patterns and designs from becoming complicated.

It is important to keep it simple when teaching beginners. So many have been discouraged over the years by "rule-based" teaching and have felt that they cannot express themselves or enjoy their hooking when there are too many rules. And they found that what was a rule with one group or teacher changed when they were with another group or teacher—conflicting messages complicate a new craft.

One of the main elements of creating simplicity in our life and in rug hooking is acceptance of both ourselves and others. Each of us has our own preferences and ways of doing things, and it is important to remember this as we learn and as we teach others.

The book began when I was commissioned by an interior designer to create a series of floor mats for a camp. They wanted very simple chevron, hit and miss, and diamond designs, motifs commonly found in early rugs. At first I was not particularly inspired by the idea, but it was a way to challenge myself by giving old motifs a modern feeling. It was a winter's work and I took it on.

As I hooked the rugs I became charmed by the simplicity of the designs and the meditative process of making them. I was brought back to the idea of just hooking a rug for the sake of the hooking itself. I loved that these rugs were going to lay on the floor, that feet would be wiped on them, dogs would lay on them, and even that they would eventually get worn out.

The experience completely changed my view of hooking as an art form. I was less worried about expressing myself and my ideas in these rugs and more concerned about making something that was both utilitarian and lovely. I came to really understand what William Morris meant when he said that everything in a home should be both functional and beautiful. Making these geometric and simply designed rugs led me to a new place in my hooking—it took me back to the basics and helped me remember that what I mostly loved about hooking rugs was the motion and the making of mats, whatever design they might be.

So these last few years I have gotten back to the basics of hooking. I am not so caught up with the art of it, or the expression of ideas, or fancy techniques. I just want to hook the mat, loop by loop, enjoying the process of it, the simplicity of it, the joy of it. I love the feeling of making a mat that will lie by my back door, and feel the everyday comings and goings of my household upon it. That in itself is enough.

- -

Facing: **Hit and Miss**

The Rug Hooker's Guide to Creativity

From every craft there grows an art

About five years ago I decided to help people become more creative in their approach to hooking rugs. Rug hooking already captivated me. I was locked into it, lured by the texture of wool, using it to express myself. I began developing a series of workshops called Color, Texture, Creativity, and Design for Hooked Mats.

When I started these workshops, teaching people how to play with texture and to hook randomly and freely, there were plenty of raised eyebrows in the class, as if to say, "I like you but I'm not sure about this." Through humor and warmth, people began to try some different textures, wider and thicker cuts of cloth, along with more loosely woven backings. When I first started working on blending creativity with rug hooking, people moved in that direction with trepidation. Most saw rug hooking strictly as a craft and had definitive ideas about technique

and the type of products that should be used. The only reason people listened to me was that some of them liked my designs and appreciated the freedom represented in them.

As rug hooking has continued to grow and many books have been written, a lot of people have picked up the craft on their own, teaching themselves in their own living rooms. There is also a wealth of information on the Internet about rug hooking, and those interested can find out about it easily. There is a great sharing of ideas and ways of making rugs that go beyond what we can learn in our own communities. I find it very interesting that, with new technology, an old idea like rug

---

The Light Falls on November, *71" x 19", #6- and #8-cut wool on burlap. Designed and hooked by Deanne Fitzpatrick, Amherst, Nova Scotia, 2003.*

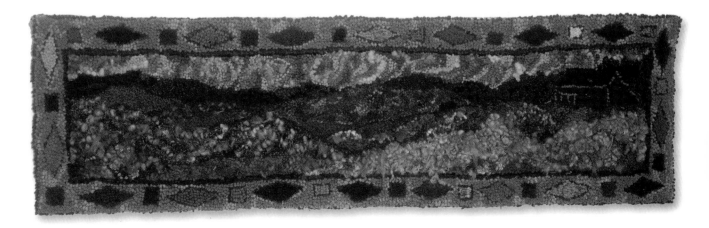

Standing Before the Monument, *8' x 6', #6- and #8-cut wool on burlap. Designed and hooked by Deanne Fitzpatrick, Amherst, Nova Scotia, 2003.*

- -

hooking has been renewed and allowed to flourish. Many people have become very interested in using rug hooking as a tool for self-expression and are open to all kinds of possibilities. These days many workshop participants come with fresh ideas and have had exposure to the idea of blending creativity and rug hooking. Whether it is adapting a stamped pattern or creating original designs, or being daring with their use of color, it seems with each passing year rug hooking is growing as an art form. The limitless possibilities offered by our minds mixing color and texture ensures its continued growth.

Primitive rug hooking is a relatively new art form when compared to drawing, painting, tapestry, sculpture, or weaving. It is a baby at 150 years old. Those of us who practice the craft are really still in the establishment phase of it—if we look at it as a medium that will continue to grow and develop over time. We have a lot to offer in this development, but we also have a lot to learn as the possibilities are explored. What an exciting prospect this is.

Forgetting Restraint and Exercising Creativity

Some people feel they have no creativity in them. This is rubbish. As my good friend says, "Gee, Deanne, I think it takes creativity to keep getting out of bed in the morning, don't you?" She sees the value in all the little things we do to keep our lives on the right track. If you have ever adapted a recipe, sung a little song, played with a child, dreamed a dream, or doodled on a piece of paper your creativity has been exercised. Granted, some people may be naturally more inclined to creative thinking, but all of us have some level of creativity within us. It is part of our humanity.

Finding the artistic rug hooker within requires an open mind and a responsive heart. It requires quiet

A Summer Turns to Fall, *60" x 36", #6- and #8-cut wool on burlap. Designed and hooked by Deanne Fitzpatrick, Amherst, Nova Scotia, 2003.*

Left: **Across the Field Towards Home**, *15" x 66", #6- and #8-cut wool on burlap. Designed and hooked by Deanne Fitzpatrick, Amherst, Nova Scotia, 2003.*

the way you feel when you paint. Rug hooking is the same—a cache of great wool, a beautiful hook with a cocobolo handle, three yards of linen, and an expensive frame does not make a rug hooker. Sitting quietly with yourself, or not so quietly with your group, and pulling the wool up through the backing makes a rug hooker. It is in the practice of making rugs that we really learn how we can approach it more creatively.

Digging for Ideas

Finding creativity should not be approached as a search but more like an archeological dig. Many of us already know how we like to create—we want to hook rugs. Knowing the medium puts you ahead of the game, since the biggest part of the creative self has already been uncovered. We have all kinds of clues around us as to what might incite us to create. It is important to ask ourselves what are our likes and dislikes? What colors make us feel good and give us energy? What ideas are important to us?

One of the biggest myths about creative people is that they gather ideas out of thin air. My own ideas grow from watching, listening, smelling, thinking, feeling, and touching. I use my senses to understand what is going on in the world. I allow whatever information that is gathered to rest in my mind, and I wait to see what happens.

time to listen to your spirit. Creativity begins with the experimentation of ideas. So the second step in becoming more artistic in your approach to rug hooking is making a commitment of time to carry out the craft. It may mean setting up a routine, so that you hook regularly, and hopefully, frequently.

One does not become a painter by simply registering with continuing education and buying $150 worth of paint and paper. The first important thing to do is to play with the paint and feel the brushes in your hand. Then start thinking about

Sometimes sketching or writing is helpful. Mostly, I remain open to the emergence of an idea. Our subconscious self is always gathering and filing away information in a kind of secret filing cabinet inside us. This information mixes with the new stimuli we are constantly getting and allows new ideas to develop.

As I go about my daily life, I remember that I am making ideas for the future. I try to live fully and see what is around me because I believe it will be important later on. Though I respond instantly to things sometimes, their inspiration does not always hold. A few weeks ago I saw the northern lights and my instant response was that would be the subject of my next rug. When I came home and finished what I had been working on, I no longer wanted to make the northern lights rug. Inspiration takes time to gestate and that idea was not ready to be born as a rug. Rainer Maria Rilke, in his book, *Letters to a Young Poet*, wrote, "Everything is gestation and then bringing forth." Our ideas fully ripen in the darkness of our subconscious, where they are lost to us, until they emerge one day as a complete surprise. Rilke suggests that an artist cannot count time because with patience our ideas will emerge freely from our soul. I agree that we must sit and wait, but, like Rilke, I do not believe we have to wait idly.

Brainstorming

The most common way of developing ideas is through brainstorming, either on your own or with a group. For example, try to think of themes for your next rug and write down every idea that comes to mind, good or bad, and generate a list to work from. If your rug-hooking group is trying to think of a title for a group show at the local museum, the same would apply, working as a group to generate a long list of possibilities. Once you come up with, and decide on an idea, share it. When inspiration is shared it just grows and grows.

- -

Dancing on Terracotta, *20" x 70", #6- and #8-cut wool on burlap. Designed and hooked by Deanne Fitzpatrick, Amherst, Nova Scotia, 2002.*

A good idea well developed is often unidentifiable from the original thought that created it. Sometimes an idea can become overdeveloped and what is needed is to get back to the roots. Do not be afraid to play with these ideas—you can always go back to the original thought.

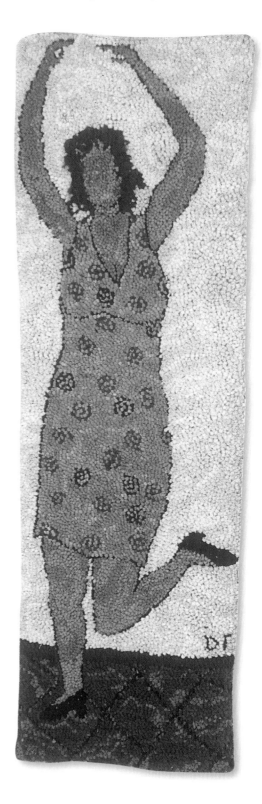

Lost in a Sea of Tea, *72" x 20", #6- and #8-cut wool on burlap. Designed and hooked by Deanne Fitzpatrick, Amherst, Nova Scotia, 1999.*

Art Creates Art

Many people feel that art creates art. Every time we create something new we have built upon the last thing we created. Sometimes I take a theme and work it in different ways as an exercise. The working of the theme can sometimes lead to new levels in your work. Other times it may lead back to the roots of it. For instance, say a night sky has been selected as a theme; try making three mats with three different night skies. Deliberately choose different wools, hook in different directions, and try to create three different effects. There is no way to do this and not learn things about hooking night skies that you did not know before. The first one may turn out to be the favorite, and this could lead you to trust your initial instincts. When a mat is finished, live with it for a while so that you can learn from it. Hang it, or place it somewhere to visit daily. Take note of your feelings when you look at it. What would you not change about it? What could you have done better? What is working in terms of color?

Journaling

The idea of keeping a creativity journal has become very popular. It is a useful tool because it is a way to reflect on your work. If we sit around and think about what we might like to express over a cup of tea, there is no record of our ideas. Often, they become lost to us. Writing down thoughts and ideas is a way of learning about yourself. Revisit these ideas months later. Creativity journals should be kept in unlined sketchbooks so there is room to draw. Rug hooking is a visual medium, and rough sketches and drawings can accompany all your notes. Do not say, "I can't draw" because I am one of those aggravating people who is going to say, "You can't draw because you don't draw." Drawing, like rug hooking, or creativity in general takes practice, and practice makes all things possible, not necessarily perfect.

When buying yourself that beautiful sketchbook full of clean white sheets, think of it as a new year in school when you first opened the new exercise books. Pick up good pencils and a basic sharpener, black ink drawing pen, and a glue stick. On the first page use the glue stick to paste in a picture of yourself as a child. I say this because small children "own" creativity. They know how to play and are uninhibited in their drawing. It is important for us to stay in touch with that part of ourselves, and to nurture it. The glue stick can also be used to paste in bits of inspiration seen in to the world around you when searching for creative rug hooking ideas. This special book can become your source book, a place to recount all the things that inspire you. Fill it with bits of fabric, art postcards, newspaper articles, personal writings and drawings, and, of course, the doodles that you did on your napkin from the luncheon meeting at work. After a little while, you can go to this book when working out a color or design problem in a rug and use it as a tool to help figure things out.

A Creative Life

As for living creatively, we all want to experience as much as we can in the one life we are graced with. Enriching our lives is our responsibility. It is an essential part of making our lives whole. There is no need to shake anything up, but there is a need to fill our lives with healthy creative ideas. Try changing your routines. If you hook in front of the television, try turning it off and listening to classical music. If you always listen to classical, try some jazz. I find that instrumental music lets me get closer to my ideas than does listening to the news.

A lot of inspiration can be gathered from going to the library and checking out a pile of big coffee table art books—not just of the familiar artists but choose some new ones. I find it fascinating how closely rug hooking approximates the brush strokes of a painter when I look at these kinds of books. Poring over books of black and white

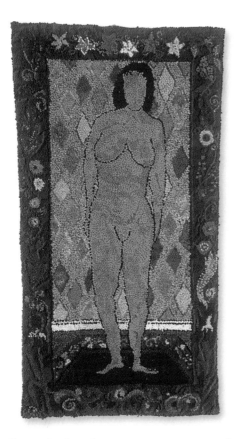

Standing Naked on the Mat, *32" x 70", #6- and #8-cut wool on burlap. Designed and hooked by Deanne Fitzpatrick, Amherst, Nova Scotia, 2002.*

Rug Hooker's
Barriers to Creativity

Some things that appear to be aids to creative thought in reality work against me. Here are some of the barriers that I have discovered:

- Keeping the same books on your bookshelves for years. Look for new ideas.
- Television, Netflix, all those distractions eat up your time. Shut off the box, turn off the screens.
- Pinterest. Seeing things on a screen is not the same as seeing it printed where you can really dwell on it. I think our brain sees it differently. Make sure you have beautiful books around that you can look at over and over again.
- Relying on your old tricks without twisting them around a bit. Try not to rely on what worked out so well the last few times you made something.
- Not exploring new materials, not adding to your stash but relying on what you know instead of what you have yet to learn.
- Sticking to the same old color palette. Color is endless and so are your options.
- Asking the same people what they think. Spread out a little and invite new and different opinions into your circle.
- Sticking with your favorite artists for inspiration. There are always new artists emerging, so make sure you explore their work too.
- Not keeping a notebook for your ideas. Make sure you use the notepad on your smartphone, even just to keep track of the things that pop into your head.
- Facebook is good for 10 to 15 minutes a day. Watch out for digital distractions like this and know that spending too much time on them might mean you are missing some valuable creative time. ■

The Long Dance, *60" x 14", #6- and #8-cut wool on burlap. Designed and hooked by Deanne Fitzpatrick, Amherst, Nova Scotia, 2002.*

photography really helps me with composition and design.

Find an art gallery close to you and make a practice of visiting it once in a while. If you can get to the city, or have access to galleries that focus on contemporary art, check out those too. It may seem those huge pieces of modern art or conceptual installations have no relevance to our simple craft, but what is relevant is the color, shape, form, and development of ideas. Once I was working with a group of modern artists at a symposium, creating art on site in a contemporary gallery. I was not quite sure why I had been chosen for the project, but I was curious and happy to be part of it. In talking with one of the artists, I said, "Sometimes I just stand in front of it and I just don't get it." The much older, well-established modern artist said, "I just stand there 'til I do." I was gently put in my place. The next time I went to see an installation, I stood there until it did make some sense to me. It did not matter what the artist's intentions had been; what mattered was my understanding of it. Do not be intimidated by it. Keep your feet firmly planted on the ground and really look at it. Whether at the Louvre smiling at Mona Lisa, or trying to figure out three stripes on a sheet of canvas, your relationship with art is your own.

Change your habits, whatever they might be. Wash the sheets, yell in the forest, smile at strangers on the street, flirt (don't go too far), stay up until midnight and howl at the full moon. Put some energy into living and that energy will emerge through your rugs.

Ideas to Nourish the Creative Genius within You

It would be so great if I could tell you that if you drink a new herbal tea and take a yoga class you would become more creative. However, we can do small activities that stretch our minds, making us more aware and receptive to creative ideas that come to us. As individuals, sketching, writing, drawing, reading, thinking, and setting up small creative challenges in our daily lives may not seem like huge steps toward hooking rugs more creatively, but they are. Each day we wake up with a bit more knowledge about ourselves, and a slightly thicker book of self-understanding. I like this self-directed approach towards creativity, but I know that there are plenty of other simple and unique ideas to push us along in our path.

Organize or Participate in a Show

Linda Rae Coughlin, in Warren, New Jersey, invited me to participate in an "Art Card" rug show (see March/April/May 2004 issue of *Rug Hooking* magazine). Linda had gotten this idea from a group of quilters who had organized a show and created a deck of cards out of art quilts. She took this idea and adapted it to rugs, inviting 53 rug-hooking artists to participate. I gladly participated for several reasons—I liked that she had the initiative to take on such a huge project and wanted to support it. I also liked the idea of making myself create a rug that I never would have thought about doing. I chose the Jack of Spades and created a very interesting rug that blended my idea with Linda's.

A second show that I have decided to submit to is Art Hits the Wall. Jan Moir, of Lunenburg County, Nova Scotia, is curating this show that asked rug hookers to create a rug based on the work of an artist or piece of work. Usually I like to come up with my own ideas and try to remain as uninfluenced as I possibly can. The "usually" is exactly why I have decided to submit to this juried show. I need to keep exploring ideas, and that sometimes means doing things that I do not see as "like me." I got out my art books, and starting sketching, not pictures of the works in them, but sketches inspired by them. I found a book of paintings by Gustav Klimt and saw a richly colored painting of a group of women all wrapped up in fabrics. It reminded me of when three or four of my sisters and I used to sleep together in the same bed. Klimt's visual image captured a memory and a feeling for me, and I had a reason to make a rug. I have just started this rug and will submit it to the jury for the show, knowing that the exercise is not in getting my work accepted, but in responding to the challenge that the show's organizers presented. If you are part of a rug-hooking group, try to work together in a brainstorming session to come up with a show theme to host at your local museum or library.

Google New Words

The next time you are surfing the Internet to find information about rug hooking, try searching some topics related to creativity to see what you find. Like rug hooking, there are tremendous amounts of information about being creative, and art in general. Some fun search words might be creativity, art rugs, fiber art, textile art, etc. There are endless combinations to explore.

Plan an Inspiration Journey

Two years ago, four artists from different disciplines and I decided to use Nova Scotia's Studio Rally map, a list of artists in the province, to plan a little studio tour for ourselves. We picked a route and organized a one-night vacation, visiting the studios of six or eight artists along the way. We have made this an annual event, finding that visiting different kinds of artists in their own studios filled us to the brim with ideas and inspiration. Check with local tourist boards for information on artists' studios in your area. They are everywhere: hidden in the hills, down by the bay, and on city streets.

Keep Inspiration Close at Hand

Try placing a bulletin board and a little shelf near where you work or spend lots of time (over the washer in the laundry room is a good place), so that you can tack up recent inspirational things. Paste them in your source book later. Things like great post cards, show invites and deadlines, paint chips, fabric swatches, sea shells, bits of branch and abandoned birds nest, a piece of moss, or an old button can be good fodder to stir up the mind. Whenever I travel I like to bring back a little found thing that helps me hold on to a memory of the place. It is often a beach rock, a shell, or a twig.

Use Nature to Color Plan

A walk in the woods or a stroll on the beach can lend some great ideas for color planning. Once while walking on a beach in Advocate, Nova Scotia, I picked up five rocks in all different colors and saw a wonderful combination of colors for an abstract rug I was working on. I happily took the rocks home as a reminder of how well planned nature actually is.

Wish Lists

Generate a wish list of things you want in your hooked rugs. How much do you want to hook? In what ways do you want your hooking to grow? What do you want to achieve with your hooking? And, what tools do you want to acquire? Be sure to check it once or twice down the road to see how you are doing.

Playful Ideas

Buy yourself a new box of crayons, make a sculpture with play dough, draw a self portrait, find a recipe with an ingredient you never used before and make it, buy a CD that you have not already heard, change the channel on the radio and turn up the volume, turn off the TV, invite someone new to dinner, swing on a swing set, write to someone you admire, kiss the cook, and think of six other possibilities that allow you to approach rug hooking and life more creatively.

Template Exercise

Give yourself a template (a simple traceable stencil) and try to think of several different designs for it. If you are part of group, try creating a set of templates (three or four) for yourselves. Let each member of the group sketch several different design possibilities and then share the ideas with each other. Another fun idea for a rug hooking group is a mat or pattern swap based on templates. Each person creates a pattern or small rug with the group's template ideas. Set a date for completion, get together, and have a pot luck supper and a swap. It gives everyone a nice memento of their rug-hooking group.

There are many ways to become more creative in our rug hooking, but the most sure-fire way is to become more creative in our daily lives, placing importance and emphasis on living artfully. The results will surely trickle down into inspiration for your hooked rugs. Remember, know yourself, waste some time, and smell the orange blossoms in the summer. They are too good to miss.

Index

Articles Originally Appearing in Rug Hooking magazine

"Rugs as Art"
Rug Hooking magazine, March/April/May 1998

"A Rug for Sophie"
Rug Hooking magazine, June/July/August 1999

"Grenfell Mats"
Rug Hooking magazine, November/December 2000

"Special Meanings in Rugs"
Rug Hooking magazine, June/July/August 2001

"Élizabeth LeFort Hansford"
Rug Hooking magazine, September/October 2002

**"Capturing the Essence:
Hooking Primitive People"**
Rug Hooking magazine, November/December 2002

"Using Templates to Create Your Own Rug"
Rug Hooking magazine, March/April/May 2004

"Rug Hooker's Guide to Creativity"
Rug Hooking magazine, June/July/August 2004

"Giving Back: Helping Your Community"
Rug Hooking magazine, June/July/August 2005

"Big Boned Girls"
Rug Hooking magazine, January/February 2009

"20 Years at the Mat"
Rug Hooking magazine, March/April/May 2010

"Hooking Skies"
Rug Hooking magazine, June/July/August 2011

"Simply Rug Hooking"
Rug Hooking magazine, March/April/May 2015

You have arrived! This sign appeared in 2016
along the Trans-Canada Highway, on the way to Amherst, Nova Scotia.

About the Author

I still live in the very farmhouse that inspired me to hook rugs and write about rug hooking over twenty-five years ago. In those years I have made over a thousand rugs and written six books, developed numerous online courses, and produced videos all about rug hooking. My first book, *Hook Me A Story*, has become a Canadian best seller and continues to be printed by Nimbus Publishing nearly twenty years after its first appearance.

I have had several solo exhibits: the Art Gallery of Nova Scotia, Acadia University Art Gallery, and The Art Gallery of Newfoundland and Labrador at the Rooms, to name a few. My work can be found in many personal and private collections, including the Canadian Museum of Civilization.

Most days you can find me in my studio in downtown Amherst, Nova Scotia, where I design rugs, make kits, dye wool, and of course, where I hook my rugs. The studio attracts visitors from all over the world. Each year I host a series of workshops and rug hooking retreats when participants come learn with me. Our workshops focus on the students' needs and abilities and I enjoy working individually with them. I enjoy teaching—it excites and energizes my own creative spirit. I love to see others grow creatively.

My website, *www.hookingrugs.com* is a hub for online learning. You can take courses from me there as well as see our full catalog of patterns, kits, and supplies. The website is full of free content on the blog and through my YouTube channel. You can learn the basics of rug hooking, take more advanced classes, download a pattern, or order wool. The website has had millions of visitors and we make updates to it on a daily basis.

I invite you to visit with me on the website—or hit the road and come visit me in person! Drop by my downtown studio for some tea and oatcakes. The sign on the highway, right before Amherst, will point you in the right direction.